A North Lancashire
Railway Album

from the cameras of Ian and Alan Pearsall

THE CALEDONIAN
46245

Leslie R Gilpin

CUMBRIAN
RAILWAYS
ASSOCIATION

Other publications by the Cumbrian Railways Association

'Cumbrian Communities' Series:
- No. 1   Grange-over-Sands *(Leslie R Gilpin)* - Out of print
- No. 2   Ravenglass *(Peter van Zeller)* - Out of print
- No. 3   Dalton-in-Furness *(Rock Battye)*
- No. 4   Whitehaven *(Howard Quayle)*
- No. 5   Millom *(Alan Atkinson)*

'Railway Histories' Series:
- The Kendal & Windermere Railway *(Dick Smith)* - Out of print
- The Furness Railway in and around Barrow *(Dr Michael Andrews)* - Out of print
- The Coniston Railway (second impression) *(Dr Michael Andrews & Geoff Holme)*
- The Track of the Ironmasters *(W McGowan Gradon - edited by Peter Robinson)*
- The Ulverstone & Lancaster Railway *(Leslie R Gilpin)*

Photographic Albums
- A Cumbrian Railway Album *(Leslie R Gilpin)*

Locomotive Histories:
- *The Great Survivor* - the rebuilding of Furness Railway No. 20 *(Tim Owen)*

Other Titles
- Railwaymen of Cumbria Remembered - A Roll of Honour

Text © 2013 Leslie R Gilpin and the Cumbrian Railways Association

Maps © Alan Johnstone and the Cumbrian Railways Association

Photographs from Cumbrian Railways Association Photo Library © The Pearsall collection

**Published by the Cumbrian Railways Association,
104 Durley Avenue, Pinner, Middlesex. HA5 1JH**

**The Association is Registered Charity No. 1025436
www.cumbrianrailways.org.uk**

Membership Secretary, Cumbrian Railways Association.
Alan Crawford, 95 Harrington Road, Workington, Cumbria CA14 2UE.

Design and layout by Michael Peascod

Printed by The Amadeus Press Ltd., Cleckheaton

ISBN 978-0-9570387-3-8

The Cumbrian Railways Association is the local railway history group for Cumbria and North Lancashire. With a membership of over 400 it is a registered charity with the aim of promoting interest in and knowledge of the railways of this area, and the part they have played in its development over the last 150 years. For more information about the Association, its activities and services, please visit our website at www.cumbrianrailways.org.uk or write to the Membership Secretary at the above address.

Contents

Front Cover
Lancaster Castle

PEQ058
18th May 1951
Preston-based ex-LMS 6P *Patriot* 4-6-0 45519 *Lady Godiva* heads south through the goods yards with the 10-40am from Glasgow Central to Manchester Victoria and Liverpool Exchange. The train is in uniform BR livery, although the tender awaits a BR Lion and Wheel roundel. The train will split at Preston with six carriages, including an ex-LMS 12-wheel dining car as fifth vehicle, heading to Manchester while the rear four will go to Liverpool. The castle and priory dominate this atmospheric view from No 2 signal box.

Title Page
Bolton-le-Sands

PEK298
27th May 1958
The Caledonian at speed. Ex-LMS 8P *Princess Coronation* 4-6-2 46245 *City of London* heads south with train W132, the 08-30am from Glasgow Central to Euston. It has just passed through Bolton-le-Sands and will soon be passing over Hest Bank troughs on its non-stop run from Carlisle to Euston. Even at this date, the Hest Bank Up Distant signal, at right, has its post painted with black and white stripes in line with former LMS practice.

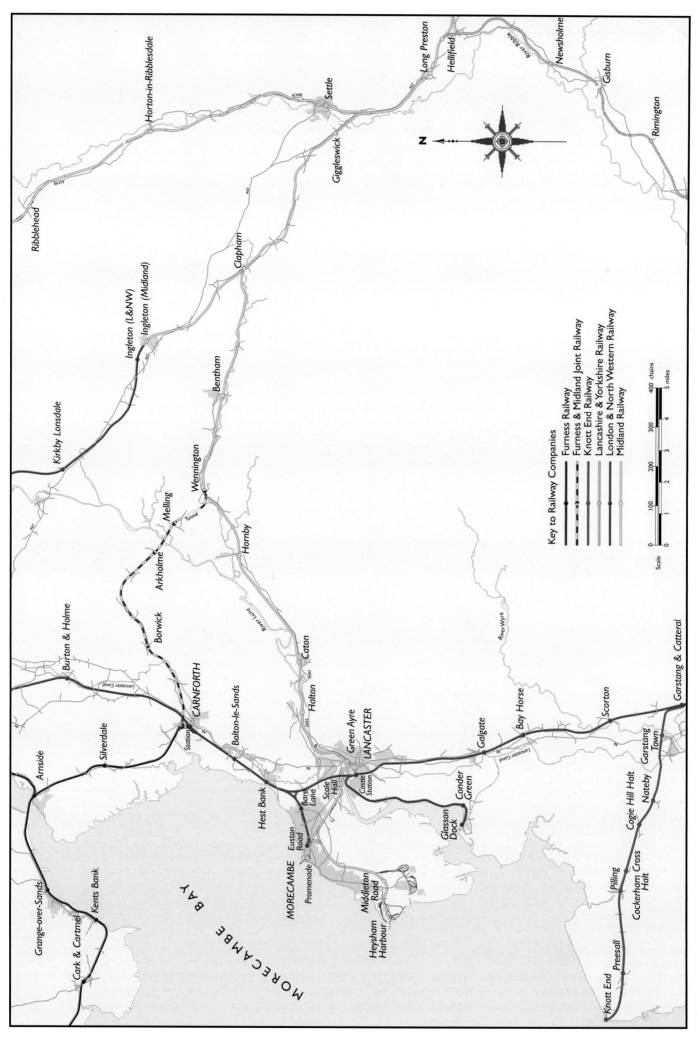

MORECAMBE BAY

Key to Railway Companies

Furness Railway
Furness & Midland Joint Railway
Knott End Railway
Lancashire & Yorkshire Railway
London & North Western Railway
Midland Railway

Scale

0   100   200   300   400 chains

0   1   2   3   4   5 miles

Introduction

THE PEARSALL brothers, Alan and Ian, were blessed as youths when their parents moved the family home to Morecambe, and less than two miles from the LMS main line to Scotland. It is no wonder that they were to spend time photographing the railway scene along not only that line but also the secondary line from Skipton to Morecambe and Heysham with its electrified section west of Lancaster. Only on the odd occasion did they venture onto the branch lines (apart from that to Morecambe Euston Road) or photograph within urban settings. For them, the countryside and lines with regular services were the places to photograph trains. The brothers also had a keen interest in shipping with the nearby port of Heysham proving a draw. It is however noticeable in the collection that they rarely photographed the industrial railway scene with the industrial lines around Lancaster and Morecambe absent. Even when they had flown the family nest they would return, often during holidays, and Alan was to maintain a retreat at Bare Lane until his death.

The brothers built up a good relationship with local railwaymen, particularly with Arthur Herbert, Bare Lane stationmaster and resident.

Ian developed his photographic technique in the Lancaster and Morecambe area and went on to become a member of Maurice W Earley's prestigious Railway Photographic Society alongside well known exponents of railway photography at the time: Eric Treacy, WJV Anderson, Derek Cross, P Ransome-Wallis and others.

This album follows on from that covering Cumbria, focusing on the area bounded by Scorton in the south, Carnforth to the north and from Heysham and Morecambe in the west to Settle Junction in the east. The Furness & Midland Joint line from Wennington to Carnforth together with the Clapham to Ingleton, Hest Bank to Morecambe and the Glasson Dock branch lines are also included.

Lancaster Castle station

PES059
6th August 1949
Ex-LMS 6P *Royal Scot* 4-6-0 46155 *The Lancer* brings the 10-10am Glasgow Central and Edinburgh Princess Street to Euston and Birmingham New Street through Castle station. On this August Saturday train W106 is running in two parts and here we see W106/1, the second part of the train, running into platform 4 instead of the through line used by the main portion of the train. The carriages are in LMS maroon while the loco has been renumbered but is generally filthy. Thus it is impossible to tell whether the tender is still in LMS livery under all the grime.

Lancaster Old Junction

PEP092
22nd June 1949

Ex-LMS 5XP 4-6-0 45543 *Home Guard* storms up the 1 in 98 of Ripley bank with an Up through goods. It has
just passed Ripley Hospital – the City of Lancaster Training College. Opened in 1864, Ripley College was built
as an endowed school for "fatherless children", and then taken over by the military in the Second World War,
before becoming a teacher training college in the initial post-war years. In 1951 it will become a secondary school.
The prefabs at right on Princess Avenue will still be standing sixty years later.

One - Final Days of the LMS and Into Nationalisation

This album starts by looking at the railway in the Lancaster area during the transition from the private London Midland & Scottish Railway to the nationalised British Railways in the latter half of the 1940s.

With the end of hostilities in Europe, restrictions on photography ended, stations regained their name boards and the new Labour government nationalised several major industries including transport "for the people". This period of hope was dampened somewhat by shortages, to some extent worse than during the war itself: the country was almost bankrupt from over six years at war, transport was worn out and fuel and food continued to be in short supply with no sign of any aid being given on the scale of that reaching the former occupied countries of Western Europe. To all intents and purposes, little really changed either in the country or on the railway.

Until the summer of 1948 the camera used for these photos was unable to 'stop' the action of moving trains very well but by the end of the year sharper results are being obtained, suggesting that either Alan or Ian had improved their technique or acquired a better camera.

Lancaster, Ladies Walk

PEA051
15th July 1947
The Last Summer of the LMS. 5MT 4-6-0 4853 passes Ladies Walk signal box with the Down Morecambe *Residential*. At one time this train from Bradford Forster Square and Leeds City (North), calling only at Lancaster Green Ayre, included a Club carriage for the worsted and woollen magnates and their managers, returning home from their mills to Morecambe. The train is passing Messrs. Standfast Dyers and Printers, whose works included the buildings of the old Lancaster Carriage and Wagon Company. The carriage and wagon works had closed in 1908 following its amalgamation with five similar companies to form the Metropolitan Amalgamated Railway Carriage and Wagon Company in 1902.

Hest Bank

PEM076
9th April 1949

Ex-LMS 4P Compound 4-4-0 1080 comes off the water troughs and approaches Hest Bank level crossing with an empty carriage working from Carnforth to Morecambe. Both locomotive and carriages are in LMS livery, although it's hard to tell whether some attempt has been made to paint out the lettering on the tender or merely clean off the dirt to reveal it. The loco from Hellifield or Manningham shed has been with its train (probably a previous working from Bradford Forster Square and Leeds City (North) to Morecambe Promenade) to Carnforth for servicing and is seen here heading to Promenade station before its return working to the West Riding.

PEK028
circa 1945

An unidentified former LNWR G2A 0-8-0 rushes south on the main line with an excursion. It appears to be carrying a reporting number CS962 and its train includes GWR vehicles at the first and sixth positions. The train is passing the signal gantry with bridge signals used (below the gantry beam rather than above) to allow sighting from approaching Down trains from beyond the nearby Marine Drive overbridge. At this time Ian Pearsall was still honing his technique in photographing moving trains. Thus whilst he has focused on the signal and the track in the foreground is sharp, Ian has been a little too quick at pressing the shutter.

Carnforth

PEK030
13th August 1945

A lovely shed scene at Carnforth with motor-fitted ex-LNWR 0-6-2T 27635 on shed at around 3-15 in the afternoon. The *Coal Tank* together with one of the 4Fs (behind) is filthy as a result of the shortage of shed staff due to the war. Whilst peace has come to Europe, there is officially one more day of hostilities in the Pacific and cleaning locomotives is a very low priority. The loco is a veteran from 1883 and will be withdrawn in March 1949 as British Railways 58894. It will be based at the former LNWR sheds at Shrewsbury and Abergavenny during the 15 months in British Railways ownership.

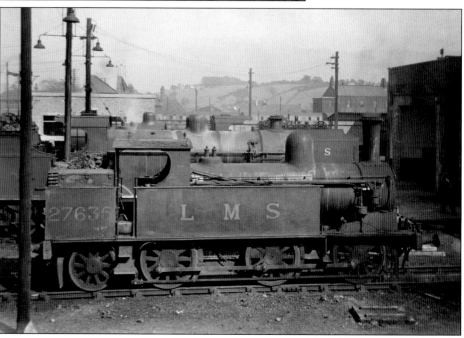

Hest Bank

PEB091
22nd August 1948
Recently rebuilt ex-LMS 6P *Patriot* 4-6-0 45512 *Bunsen* brings the 10-05am Glasgow Central to Birmingham New Street train into Hest Bank. The Up line is being relaid causing the train to have worked wrong line from Carnforth. 45512 is allocated to Carlisle, Upperby shed and had only come out of the works after rebuilding in the previous month. Although it carries a BR smokebox number (with numerals in LMS Sans Serif type) it has yet to receive its shed code and smoke deflectors. In fact it is hard to tell if it has actually received its final coat of paint.

PEP098
Sunday 26th June 1949
Still in its LMS livery, 5MT 4-6-0 4905 restarts a Barrow Central to Euston train from Hest Bank. The nine-coach train had stopped short in the station due to engineering works on the Down line. Single line working is in operation from here to either Morecambe South Junction or possibly Lancaster No 4 signal box. Shirtsleeves appear to be the order of the day for the people on the footbridge. Hest Bank was a popular place for spotters, and parents showing their children the trains. As is well known, this is the point where the West Coast main line briefly passes the sea and its shore was always busy in the summer. The station staff have made a start on tidying up the station gardens by writing out the station name in white-painted stones.

Hest Bank

PEP099
26th June 1949
Ex-LMS 5XP *Jubilee* 4-6-0 45678 *De Robeck* brings a Euston to Glasgow Central relief train slowly on the Up line into Hest Bank during track renewal works. The loco has received its British Railways livery but is already filthy through lack of cleaning. The leading carriages of the 14-carriage train, much cleaner than the locomotive, are still in LMS livery. The Down line has been relaid and the platelayers are installing a new crossing giving access onto the Morecambe branch. Note the complete absence of aerials on the roofs in the background. This is the golden age of the radio; the BBC would not broadcast television across Lancashire for another two years.

PES011
26 June 1949
The signalman watches as ex-LMS 7P *Princess Coronation* 4-6-2 46237 *City of Bristol* edges past the engineering works with the Down *Royal Scot*. Both loco and tender are in LMS 1946 livery, apart from a new numberplate with sans serif numerals (except for the prefix 4) and a number 4 judiciously added to the LMS number on the cab side. The carriages, however, sport the new Crimson and Cream livery as befits the premier train of the London Midland Region. The LNWR-built signalbox has another eight years of life ahead of it. In December 1958 it will be replaced by a new box located to the north of the level crossing. Note the token collector at right: the branch from Bare Lane is controlled at this time by electric token.

Morecambe, Schola Green Lane

PEO028/1
1948
Under the wires at Morecambe. British Railways-built Black 5 4-6-0 44756 throws black smoke (despite the 6.6Kv wires running above) as it approaches Schola Green Lane crossing, soon after leaving Morecambe Promenade for Leeds City (North). The loco is new, being one of those built with Caprotti rotary valve gear. Built in the first months of the British Railways era when decisions were yet to be made on liveries, 44756 has received a London Midland Region prefix on what is otherwise an LMS serif-style number plate. Otherwise the loco carries little to indicate that it is a British Railways loco. The carriages, however, are in a mix of LMS and BR liveries. Despite being fitted with electric head code lamps, 44756 carries oil lamps on the buffer beam. Meanwhile, 4F 0-6-0 44467 at the right has received its British Railways insignia. It is standing at Euston Road station, possibly on the turntable there. The line to Torrisholme No 2 Junction and Heysham is out of view, to the left.

Morecambe, Euston Road

PEP095
25th June 1949
Train W519, headed by ex-LMS 5MT 4-6-0 M5374, makes a spirited start from Euston Road with the 11-55am excursion from Morecambe Euston Road to Oldham. This would be returning holidaymakers who had taken advantage of the first week of Oldham's Wakes Weeks (the two weeks commencing on the penultimate Saturday in June) with a stay at the seaside. Apart from the M suffix on the loco cab side, this train appears to be completely in LMS livery. The train is crossing onto the Up line. The Down line runs into Euston Road with a crossing, behind the photographer, allowing trains for Promenade station to access the nearest track. This continues for a distance towards Bare Lane as a headshunt known as York Siding. To the left of the train can be seen Euston Road signal box and the catenary masts on the former Midland Railway approach to Promenade.

Lancaster Old Junction

PEP093
22nd June 1949
About to crest Ripley bank is ex-WD 2-8-0 90331 with the 3-30pm Heysham to Preston goods train. As this train reversed at Morecambe Promenade to gain access to the former LNWR lines, it had a brake van at both front and rear of the train. The train is passing the former LNWR loco shed as it approaches Lancaster No 1 box, also known as Old Junction. The shed was known variously as Bridge Road, Ripley or, more colloquially, "Dog Kennel" shed. Only the rear part of the shed still stands, with its water tank and shed office alongside. Careful examination of the photograph reveals the impression of the demolished 2-bay roof on the front of the water tank. "Dog Kennel" shed closed from 4th February 1934 and the main length of the shed, track work and turntable were removed before the outbreak of war.

PEP094
22nd June 1949
Ex-LMS 5MT 4-6-0 45185 passes Lancaster No.1 signal box with an unidentified up Class H through goods train. To its right is the line to Lancaster Old Goods: the Lancaster & Preston Junction Railway line to the original Lancaster terminus. The LPJR passenger station closed in August 1849, some three years after the opening of the line to Castle Station and Carlisle. During that time both the LPJR and Lancaster & Carlisle Railway ran trains from their own respective stations in Lancaster over the line to Preston. This ceased not long after the sale of the line to the Lancaster & Carlisle company. The LPJR passenger station and offices were eventually sold off, the offices now forming part of Lancaster General Hospital. The goods facilities and one-time loco shed (itself replaced by Dog Kennel shed) were retained. The line will remain open to serve the goods yard until their closure in 1967.

Lancaster Castle

PES015
1st July 1949
Six-week old Ivatt 4MT 2-6-0 43034 runs tender-first across the junction from the Down platform line onto the Glasson Dock branch, devoid of any head or tail lamp. It is possibly on its way to platform 1 or 2, behind the photographer, to take a train to Morecambe, Euston Road. This loco was delivered new from Horwich works to Green Ayre shed. Beyond No 4 signalbox stands a rake of three non-corridor carriages. Perhaps these form a second train set for busy times on the Euston Road services. As will be seen, the loco will later return to Lancaster with the 5-20pm from Euston Road to Preston. The photographer, standing at the end of platform 1, has turned an otherwise standard three-quarter view of the loco into a portrait by simply including so much of the surrounding infrastructure and scenery.

PEB050
19th July 1948
Midland Railway-built electric motor car 28612 of 1908 stands ready to propel its LMS-built driving trailer, 22202, away from platform 6 at Castle station with the 2-15pm train to Morecambe Promenade. The motor car is still in LMS maroon livery with simple lining. Despite the route being electrified for forty years, the LMS still saw fit to retain the large warning board alongside the pantograph and other roof-mounted electrical equipment. Note how the LMS had filled an otherwise empty poster board at right by simply using it to name the location; LMS Lancaster Castle Station.

Lancaster Castle

PES022
1st July 1949
On the south side of Castle station, Ivatt 4MT 2-6-0 43034 heads the 5-20pm Morecambe Euston Road to Preston train past No 3 signalbox. The signalman is lowering the starter signal as the train accelerates away. The train itself appears to be the normal three-carriage non-corridor set used on the Euston Road to Lancaster Castle shuttles strengthened with a non-corridor third. The cattle wagons in the dock at right are of interest with four or five different designs within the seven-wagon rake. The track in that siding is coated in lime, spilled from cattle wagons interiors during re-liming. The walls of these wagons were painted in lime between use to avoid the spread of disease. The ancient walls of Lancaster Castle itself can be seen against the skyline.

PES019
1st July 1949
Train W220, from Windermere to Preston, rolls slowly off Carlisle Bridge and into Castle station behind ex-LMS Fowler 4MT 2-6-4T 42314. The train has been brought in "under signals" by the signalman at No. 4 box and is now routed into Platform 5. 42314 has received its BR number and "BRITISH RAILWAYS" lettering on the tank sides. Curiously, the letter S is an afterthought, actually looking as if the painter has made use of a spare LMS transfer or even retained the last initial of the former LMS insignia. The train, however, is a mixture of stock in LMS livery.

PES017
1st July 1949
At around 4-00pm on a brilliant summer afternoon, pioneer ex-LMS 7P *Princess Royal* 4-6-2 46200, *The Princess Royal* pulls away from Castle station with the train W251. This is the 10-40am Euston to Carlisle, Windermere and Barrow Central: the Barrow portion has been detached and left in Platform 3. With a temporary speed restriction just ahead, the *Princess* has a clear exhaust and is producing no smoke as it draws its lightened load towards Carlisle Bridge and the north. Although 46200 has received its BR number, its tender and carriages retain LMS livery.

PES018
1st July 1949
Soon after departure of the Carlisle and Windermere portion of train W251, ex-LMS 5MT 4-6-0 45343 draws the through carriages, now strengthened to become the 4-08pm train to Barrow Central, towards Carlisle Bridge. The *Black 5* is in the grimy black livery typical of the post-war years. Although it has received its BR number, it is impossible to make out any BR identity on the tender. The train is made up of a mixed selection of stock in LMS livery. Permanent way work must be underway on the Down line on Carlisle Bridge; the train is passing a speed restriction board and sleepers and chairs are piled up on the line side.

Scorton, Wyre Bridge

PEG246
26th August 1954

At probably the most picturesque spot on the Lancaster & Preston Junction line, ex-LMS 5MT 4-6-0 45291 rushes across the six-arch viaduct over the River Wyre with train W201, the 2-45pm from Preston to Barrow Central. Cartographers from the Ordnance Survey named this "Wyre Bridge" but the locals still call it the "Six Arches".

Two - The LNWR:
To Lancaster from the South

WHEN BUILT, the Lancaster & Preston Junction Railway was a bad railway, a very bad railway. Despite being engineered on a fairly straight and level line, opening in June 1840, it was emasculated by the resignation of all but one of its directors a year after opening, allowing itself to be bullied by its neighbour to the south, the North Union Railway. The LPJR was almost deprived of free access into the NUR station at Preston and the main line south to London, and became subject to a dubious lease from its near neighbour and competitor, the Lancaster Canal! What other railway in the country could have been subject to fierce competition, even for passenger traffic, from a canal company? Thus by the time of the opening of the Lancaster & Carlisle Railway, the LPJR had become ramshackle: signalling involved the use of flags at the stations, often wrapped around the flagpoles, ballasting was said to be done using a wagon on the back of passenger trains and the rolling stock was slowly becoming rotten through lack of maintenance. The situation was compounded by the LCR running its own trains non-stop from Lancaster Castle, from September 1846, onto the LPJR at what became known as Lancaster Old Junction, through to Preston.

Meanwhile the LPJR continued to run its trains from its Lancaster terminus on Penny Street to its own terminus at Preston. All came to a head with the inevitable accident, at Bay Horse station on 21st August 1848, when protected only by a flag signal (literally a flag raised up a pole but only visible in a wind), the 3-45 pm LPJR Preston-Lancaster local was struck in the rear by the LCR's late-running 9-00am Euston-Glasgow express.

Of course all that was but a memory, and when the Pearsalls came to photograph along the line all had changed. Bury 0-4-0s and LNWR 2-2-0s and 2-4-0s, running unregulated, had been replaced by Stanier Pacifics, *Black 5*s and even first generation diesels running along a 90mph racetrack. The only drawback one observes in their photographs along this section is the scenery, or rather lack of it. The expansive views along the Settle to Carlisle line or on the line over Shap were absent. The line ran along the plain between the Forest of Bowland and the expanse of the Fylde with few opportunities to take more than the classic "three-quarter" shot, favoured by railway photographers of the day. However, our photographer brothers took what advantage they could, especially of the frequent services along the line.

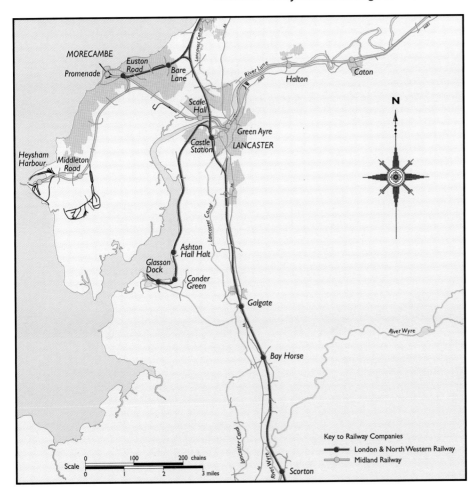

Scorton

PEG249
26th August 1954

Ex-LMS 8P *Princess Coronation* 4-6-2 46254 *City of Stoke-on-Trent* roars through Woodacres Great Wood towards Scorton with train W251, the 10-40am from Euston to Carlisle. The twelve-carriage train appears to be made up completely of LMS-design stock in uniform crimson and cream livery. The train will split at Lancaster with through carriages for the Furness line being dropped off.

PEG248
26th August 1954
BR 6MT *Clan* 4-6-2 72000 *Clan Buchanan* approaches the bridge over Gubberford Lane with train C400, the 2-15pm from Manchester Victoria to Glasgow Central, with portions from Liverpool Exchange and for Edinburgh Princes Street. Woodacres Great Wood is in the distance. Today the M6 runs parallel to the railway southwards from here, tearing a swathe from the woodland and marring the view over the fields to the left. These workings were always heavily loaded, and this one is no exception, with thirteen carriages behind the loco.

PEG247
26th August 1954
LMS 6P *Jubilee* 4-6-0 45671 *Prince Rupert* crosses Gubberford Lane with the 10-50am Glasgow Central to Manchester Victoria train. Scorton station had stood on the embankment in the distance until closure from 1st May 1939. The signalbox had been closed in December 1932, when the LMS introduced Intermediate Block Signals. That seen to the left of the train is Garstang & Catterall Down IBS No 2.

PEG251
26th August 1954
Ex-LMS 5MT 4-6-0 45314 hauls an Up Class H through freight along the embankment to the south of the site of Scorton Station. Of the 30-odd wagons in the train, there are a few cattle wagons and at least one bogie-bolster but general loads are largely carried under tarpaulins in open wagons with only a handful of vans used.

Bay Horse

PEJ405
3rd April 1956
Ex-LMS 6P *Patriot* 4-6-0 45504 *Royal Signals* passes through Bay Horse with train W512, the 1-00pm relief from Carlisle to Manchester. Being the Tuesday following the Easter holiday, this train was probably laid on to handle Lancastrian holidaymakers returning from a visit to the Border City or the northern and eastern Lake District. Despite having smoke deflectors, smoke drifts down alongside the smokebox and in front of the chimney. Perhaps the train is not running particularly fast.

PEJ404
3rd April 1956
Named after the adjacent inn, Bay Horse was the site of the collision between a Euston to Glasgow express and a LPJR stopping train on 21st August 1848. By 1956 this is one of the two remaining passenger stations between Preston and Lancaster. This view captures the original LPJR station house with its deep bay window and LNWR extensions, low platforms and the LNWR-designed station master's house in the distance. Only the oil lamps, a couple of enamel signs advertising Virol and a solitary poster inviting travel to Ireland can be seen to suggest that the station may be open. Up until closure it was served by four or five trains in each direction but none on Sundays. Bay Horse will close after the departure of the last train on 11th June 1960.

PEG643
3rd April 1956
Ex-LMS 5MT 4-6-0 45069 heads north with train W201, the 2-40pm train from Preston to Barrow Central, after passing through Bay Horse station. The station master's house can seen in distance. Despite being a relatively local journey, at 55¾ miles, the train is running under a Class A (express) headcode.

PEG639
3rd April 1956
Ex-LMS 5MT 4-6-0 44870 speeds south towards Bay Horse with train W535, a Workington Main to Manchester relief working. Traffic expectations must have been high on this, the Tuesday after the Easter weekend holiday. This train would carry returning holidaymakers from their break in West Cumberland or the western and southern Lake District to south-east Lancashire. The colour-light signal in the distance is the Down Intermediate Block signal controlled from Bay Horse.

Bay Horse

PEG645
3rd April 1956

Lit by the afternoon sunshine, ex-LMS 6P *Jubilee* 4-6-0 45645 *Collingwood* rushes south towards Bay Horse station with an unidentified train. It is possible that this is train W266, the 2-30pm from Morecambe Euston Road to Crewe, in which case *Collingwood* will have picked up this train at Lancaster Castle, after previously piloting train W254, the 10-50am from Workington Main - Preston, from Barrow (departing 1-00pm, see opposite). This was a running-in turn for locomotives out of Crewe Works and popular with local enthusiasts because of the variety of locos that appeared.

PEG638
3rd April 1956
Ex-LMS 8P *Princess Coronation* 4-6-2 46242 *City of Glasgow* and train W98, the 10-05am Glasgow Central to Birmingham New Street, speeds towards Bay Horse station on its non-stop run from Carlisle to Crewe. This is quite a lengthy train, with 14 carriages and possibly a van, but just within the limits for a Limited Load train for an 8P loco (560 tons from Carlisle to Shap).

PEG640
3rd April 1956
Ex-LMS 5MT 4-6-0 45409 approaches Bay Horse with train W254, the 10-50am from Workington Main and 1-00pm from Barrow Central to Preston. This impressive train of 12 carriages, of assorted LMS designs, would have been double-headed over the Furness line and as far Lancaster Castle, with 45645 *Collingwood* assisting 45409 on this particular day (see opposite). It carries through carriages for Euston, which will be shunted into train W110, the 9-00am ex-Perth, during the latter train's nine minute lay-over at Preston.

PEG245
26th August 1954
Ex-LMS 8P *Princess Coronation* 4-6-2 46229, *Duchess of Hamilton,* with the 9-00am from Perth to Euston. Train W110 is passing under Hampson Lane, to the north of Bay Horse. Its train of eight carriages and a van mirrors the size of the named expresses between Euston and Scotland of the period. The *Duchess* and train is running behind train W254 (above) where it will pick up the through carriages from Workington.

Lancaster Castle

PEG602
3rd September 1955
5-45pm on a warm clear evening and ex-LMS 8P *Princess Royal* 4-6-2 46212 *Duchess of Kent* approaches Lancaster No 2 signal box showing a clear exhaust and a little steam from the safety valves. This is train W97, the *Mid-Day Scot*, which left Euston at 1-30pm with stops only at Rugby, Crewe and Carlisle before its arrival in Glasgow. Unusually, *Duchess of Kent*, the last of her class to be built, isn't carrying a headboard.

PEF405
13th September 1952
The driver has really opened up ex-LMS 5MT 4-6-0 45294 as it passes Lancaster No 2 signal box with an Up goods train. The bark of the exhaust must have been heard all across Lancaster. Note the poles piled up at right beyond the yard lamp. It is difficult to work out whether these are telegraph poles or masts for use on the Lancaster – Morecambe – Heysham electrification which was being re-equiped at this time. Curiously many of the poles have the number '28' on the end.

PEQ059
18th May 1951
Former War Department (WD) 2-8-0 90640 heads south towards Lancaster No 2 signalbox with the 3-30pm Heysham to Lostock Hall goods. Unlike many locos at this time, the 2-8-0 is remarkably clean and perhaps recently repainted. The leading brake van has the letters "LMS" painted out whilst the odd wagon still retains that lettering. In the Up sidings some shunting is underway with the shunter applying the handbrake on an ex-Private Owner wagon.

PEF415
17th September 1952
Ex-LMS 8P *Princess Coronation* 4-6-2 46225 *Duchess of Gloucester* starts out of Lancaster with steam to spare as it approaches No 2 signal box with the Up *Mid-Day Scot*. Usually the *Mid-Day Scot* would run non-stop from Carlisle and not call at Lancaster but here we see the train leaving Platform 4, there being an unidentified tank engine stood close to No. 3 box waiting for the signal for the Up through line. If the *Mid-Day Scot* was on time, it would pass Lancaster at about 4-50pm when an afternoon train from Workington Main to Manchester would be in Platform 4. The *Scot* must be late! The leading carriage is a Thompson LNER design full brake with the second vehicle still in LMS maroon.

PEF416
17th September 1952
A beautifully lit shot of BR-built Fairburn 4MT 2-6-4T 42135 from Green Ayre shed with the 5-20pm train from Morecambe Euston Road to Preston, viewed from No. 2 signal box. The tank engine seen in PEF415 is still blocking the Up through line close to No 3 box. The cattle wagons in the siding behind the loco seem to have livestock in them. 42135 had been delivered new to Green Ayre in 1950 and stayed there until 1962 when it was reallocated to Wigan.

Lancaster Castle

PEF422
20th September 1952
The old and the new on the Manchester express. Ex-MR 2P 4-4-0 40356 pilots BR 6MT 4-6-2 72007 *Clan Mackintosh* as they start from Castle station with the 10-30am train from Glasgow to Manchester. While the *Clan*, from Kingmoor shed, is only six months old, the 2P from Upperby dates from 1883, although it had been rebuilt a few times in the intervening years, appearing in this superheated form before the Great War. Also in this view from No 2 signal box, ex-LMS 4F 0-6-0 44032 from Green Ayre shed shunts the goods shed roads.

PEG569
3rd September 1955
Seen from Lancaster No 2 signal box, ex-LMS 2P 4-4-0 40660 pilots ex-LMS 7P *Rebuilt Scot* 4-6-0 46136 *The Border Regiment* on train W484, the 12-15pm from Perth to Euston, away from its stop at Lancaster. Although the *Scot* has been rebuilt, technically it is the older – by three years – of the locos seen here. Being the last holiday weekend of the season, lack of space at Morecambe has meant five sets of excursion stock have had to be brought here for stabling before being returned later in the evening.

PEF404
13th September 1952
A lovely view of ex-LMS 6P *Jubilee* 4-6-0 45720 *Indomitable* of Patricroft shed accelerating out of platform 4 with train W70 from Barrow Central to Euston. It is a clear day but there seems to be enough of a breeze to catch the exhaust. Note the yard crane adjacent to the goods shed on the Up side: even at a centre like Lancaster, a hand crane was the best the railway could provide for handling larger items and perhaps demonstrates one of the reasons why the railway couldn't compete for smaller goods with the roads.

PEB144
3rd January 1953
A cold, dank day at Lancaster when the low sun has failed to warm the frost from the sleepers. Peppercorn A1 4-6-2 60152 *Holyrood* approaches Lancaster No. 3 box at speed with a Birmingham New Street to Glasgow express (see also Chapter 3). The loco is possibly still in the standard passenger locomotive blue livery. The open wagons outside the goods shed are loaded with a variety of 'less than wagon-load' goods unprotected from the weather. The signalman at No 3 box appears unconcerned about the weather and has a window open; perhaps his stove was smoking into the operating floor.

Lancaster Castle

PED087
10th March 1951

A schoolboy spotter pays close attention as ex-LMS *Crab* 5MT 2-6-0 42895 of Green Ayre shed backs onto its train in platform 4 with steam to spare. On this occasion the 1-20pm train from Morecambe Euston Road to Lancaster Castle has been extended to Preston in connection with a football match at Preston North End's Deepdale ground. The 1950-51 season is particularly good for the Preston team: they will become Second Division champions and be promoted to the First Division. However our school lad appears more interested in the *Crab* than going to the match. Note the unusual headlamp above the left hand buffer.

PEC853
2nd August 1952
LMS 7P *Royal Scot* 4-6-0 46134 *The Cheshire Regiment* rolls into Lancaster Castle with train W74, the 8-20am from Carlisle to London, as a parcels train heads north. 46134 is still in its original BRITISH RAILWAYS livery while the second carriage retains LMS red. The electrified branch to Green Ayre falls away to the right, the Midland timber and steel portals giving way to more substantial catenary as it enters former LNWR property. The splitting signals above 46134 show it is running into platform 4 whilst the others protect the roads into platforms 5 and 6. The Distant signals are for Lancaster No 3 whilst the calling-on arms indicate that shunting also occurred in these platforms.

PEO030
9th September 1950
Viewed from West Road, 8P *Princess Coronation* 4-6-2 46253 *City of St Albans* thunders through Castle station with the 8-40am from Perth to Euston, train W110. The majority of carriages appear to be still in LMS livery although the second has received Crimson and Cream. Whilst 46253 has received a circular smokebox, the running boards still curve inwards below the smoke deflectors, indicating that this was once a streamlined loco. A loco crew watch from beneath an LMS *Hawkseye* nameboard, still with its original reflective yellow finish.

PEG760
21st July 1956
Ex-LMS 8P *Princess Coronation* 4-6-2 46229 *Duchess of Hamilton* storms through Lancaster with the Down *Royal Scot* while 46222 *Queen Mary* stands in Platform 3 with train W67, the 11-25am from Birmingham New Street to Glasgow Central as the spotters look on. The *Royal Scot* is running about 15 minutes late causing the Birmingham train, which is booked to follow non-stop through Lancaster, to be held in platform 3. The *Duchess* will retain her 'semi' smokebox for another six months whilst *Queen Mary* has had a normal smokebox for almost three years.

Lancaster Castle

PEF572
19th April 1953

Excursion stock for train C883 is set back into platform 6 by an unidentified loco whilst a train crew walk down the branch to Green Ayre shed. There is plenty of incidental detail in this photo: the carriages correctly labelled at the ends with the train number (obligatory on a Saturday), the catenary – of steel construction within LNWR property but with wooden masts once on the Midland - and the signals controlling the lines into platforms 4, 5 and 6, with Distant arms for No 3 box signals and calling-on arms. Curiously the train is being controlled by the Up Home signal for platform 6 and not by the calling-on arm.

PEQ057
18th May 1951
Pioneer 1,600 horsepower Co-Co diesels 10000 and 10001 lean into the curve of the through line with the Up *Royal Scot*. Both diesels are in original black livery, 10000 still with its LMS lettering. As the London Midland Region premier train, carriages are predominantly brand new Mark 1s and all carry Crimson and Cream livery. In the distance, beyond No. 4 signal box, the rake of three non-corridor carriages is being shunted, perhaps to form the next local train to Morecambe Euston Road.

PEK702
31st July 1959
With a year of operating life remaining, 57 year-old ex-MR 3F 0-6-0 43749 has steam to spare as it awaits the signal to proceed over the Up through line with a Class F express unfitted Up train of empty mineral wagons. New BR steel coal wagons are predominant but two ex-Private Owner wooden body wagons are at the front of the train. A northbound passenger train is heading off into the distance. 43749 was based at Sheffield Grimesthorpe throughout its BR career. This suggests that the train is either from Roosecote, Barrow or Willowholme, Carlisle power stations and returning to the South Yorkshire coalfield via Preston.

Bolton-le-Sands

PEJ989
8th September 1957

Under an atmospheric Sunday afternoon sky, ex-LMS 6P Jubilee 4-6-0 45625 *Sarawak* cruises southwards from Bolton-le-Sands on its non-stop run from Carlisle to Crewe. The 10-00am Glasgow-Euston *Royal Scot*, train W136, is made up of a uniform consist of thirteen maroon Mark I carriages. A Jubilee on this train is most unusual, the normal motive power being a *Princess Coronation Pacific*.

Three - The LNWR:
North from Lancaster

UNLIKE ITS neighbour immediately to the south, the Lancaster & Carlisle Railway was a well-managed railway, although heavily influenced during its independent life by the company owning a major part of its shares, the LNWR. Whilst well known for its hilly route between Carnforth and Penrith, the line north of the river Lune to Carnforth was of modest gradients as it dropped gently past Morecambe South Junction and Hest Bank

to a level section on to Bolton-le-Sands before climbing into Carnforth. Trains pass along the coastal plain, reaching the sea at Hest Bank, with its camping coaches and fleeting views across Morecambe Bay to the Lake District mountains. Not far to the east the A6 winds through Slyne and Bolton-le-Sands, carrying the growing motor traffic from the south to Scotland, whilst the Lancaster Canal follows a higher contour.

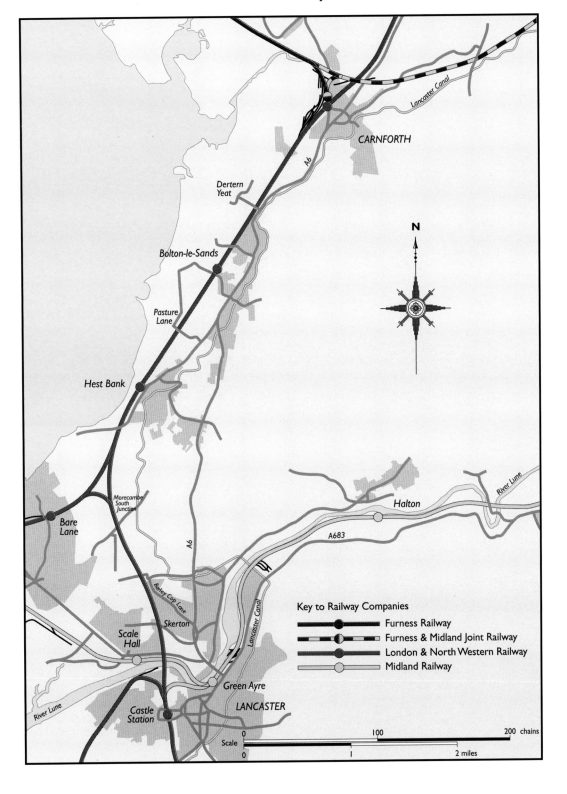

Key to Railway Companies
- Furness Railway
- Furness & Midland Joint Railway
- London & North Western Railway
- Midland Railway

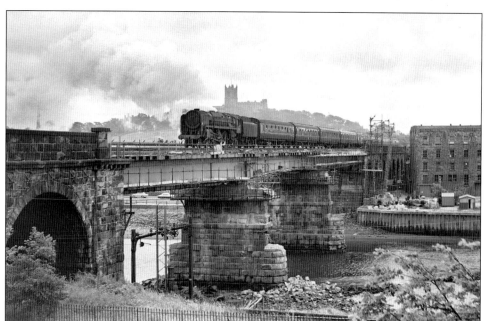

Lancaster, Carlisle Bridge

PEH966
10th July 1963
During 1963 British Railways rebuilt Carlisle Bridge, replacing the large girders, which once hid trains from view with the modern structure, which remains today. This was not a straightforward task as much of the work of lowering the bridge piers and other work was done without diverting trains. Only when the main girders were lifted into position, from the depot set up on St Georges Quay on the far bank of the Lune, did trains get diverted via Green Ayre and Morecambe Promenade. Here BR 7MT *Britannia* 4-6-2 70044 *Earl Haig* heads the 3-55pm from Manchester to Barrow.

Lancaster, Skerton

PEK355
21st July 1958
With Lancaster Castle and Priory in the distance, ex-LMS 4MT Fowler 2-6-4T 42332 accelerates train C406, the 5-45pm from Liverpool Exchange to Whitehaven Corkickle over Torrisholme Road, Skerton. The train is made up of an interesting mix of LMS-designed corridor carriages. That this train is to Corkickle and not Whitehaven Bransty is interesting: Whitehaven Tunnel, between the two stations, had been closed overnight since the 1930s to allow a slow process of rebuilding and was formally reopened on 29th June 1958. Perhaps some finishing work was still required in the following weeks.

PEK356
21st July 1958
Monday is washing day and the housewives living on Granville Road are taking advantage of the evening air with their washing still out at 8 o'clock! The safety valves are blowing as ex-LMS 8P *Princess Coronation* 4-6-2 46245 *City of London* passes Skerton, still within sight of Lancaster Castle and Priory. Train W143, *The Caledonian*, had left Euston at 4-15pm for Glasgow Central, and will have passed through Lancaster Castle at 7-57pm, helped by its limited load of 270 tons or 8 carriages and few stops en route.

Lancaster, Barley Cop Lane

PEG211
31st July 1954
On a warm July afternoon ex-LMS 4P Compound 4-4-0 41187 piloting ex-LMS 6P *Jubilee* 4-6-0 45717 *Dauntless* head towards Lancaster Castle on train W270, the 9-26am from Perth to Manchester. Our photographer has climbed up the embankment beside the bridge over Barley Cop lane to capture this view. Note the immaculate workmanship of the track gang on this length: well mown embankments and ballast in line along the cess. The signal wire is for Morecambe South Junction's Down Distant signal.

PEK354
21st July 1958
On a bright July evening ex-LMS 8P *Princess Coronation* 4-6-2 46223 *Princess Alice* rushes towards Lancaster with the 3-00pm from Glasgow Central to Euston, *The Caledonian*. The train has just passed over Barley Cop Lane and will soon be passing Skerton before crossing the Lune and speeding through Castle station.

Lancaster, Barley Cop Lane

PEB215
24th March 1953
The 10-50am from Workington Main to Preston train was almost guaranteed to be double headed from Barrow. Ex-LMS 7P *Rebuilt Scot* 4-6-0 46112 *Sherwood Forester* pilots ex-LMS 6P *Patriot* 4-6-0 45537 *Private E Sykes, V.C.* on train W254. The third carriage on the train is still in LMS red, even five years after Nationalisation. As mentioned elsewhere, the pilot for this train was a running-in turn from Crewe; in this case the *Scot* is normally based at Leeds Holbeck. Through carriages from this train will be added at Preston onto the 9-00am train ex-Perth to Euston.

PEB218
26th March 1953
Ex-LMS 6P *Patriot* 4-6-0 45550, with a Fowler high-sided tender, crosses Barley Cop lane with an Up express cattle train, probably from Heysham. The train is running with a Class D head code, indicating at least 30% of the cattle wagons are fitted with vacuum brakes. The train formation includes an interesting variety of wagon designs, plus a brake van mid-train as well as at the rear, suggesting that the train has or will run in two portions at some point.

PEB219
26th March 1953
BR Peppercorn A1 4-6-2 60152 *Holyrood* leaves the northern suburbs of Lancaster with train W67, the 11-25am Birmingham New Street to Glasgow Central. Although the train is composed almost entirely of LMS-design carriages, the leading full brake is of ex-GWR Hawksworth design, a through carriage from Bristol or the West of England. For almost two years several locos of this class were based at Polmadie, Glasgow and worked trains over the WCML at least as far south as Crewe.

PEB220
26th March 1953
LMS 6P *Patriot* 4-6-0 45502 *Royal Naval Division* heads a Down "Maltese Cross" express goods train north from Lancaster; the rear of the train is crossing Barley Cop Lane. The four fitted vans at the front of the train allow it to run as a Class E train, the remaining wagons being largely without vacuum brakes. For many years these trains were annotated with a Maltese Cross symbol in the working timetable.

Morecambe South Junction

PEB671
Saturday 1st August 1953
BR 4MT 4-6-0 75012 rolls over Morecambe South Junction with train W278, the 11-15am Workington Main to Manchester Victoria. Typical of the time, the carriages in this train are from a variety of designs. Morecambe South Junction signal box dates from 1888 and was built for the opening of the curve from here to Bare Lane in May of that year. The loco has lost its shed plate at some point.

PEB673
Saturday 1st August 1953
The fireman of ex-LMS 2P 4-4-0 40565 leans out of the cab, proud of the black smoke he has created for our photographer. Preston-based 40565 is piloting ex-LMS 6P *Jubilee* 4-6-0 45698 *Mars* of Liverpool, Bank Hall, as they reach Morecambe South Junction with the 1-36pm from Carlisle to Manchester, train W270.

PES245
3rd April 1961
The crew of ex-LMS 7P *Rebuilt Patriot* 4-6-0 45512 *Bunsen* create some black smoke for the photographer as it thunders towards Morecambe South Junction. 45512 is heading north with train C402, the 4-10pm from Liverpool Exchange to Glasgow Central. The leading carriage is a GWR design appropriately in Western Region Chocolate & Cream livery while the remainder are in Maroon. The northernmost houses of Skerton can be seen in background.

PEB672
7th August 1953
The carriages are glinting in the bright August sunshine in comparison to the grimy BR 6MT *Clan* 4-6-2 72000 *Clan Buchanan* as train C392, the 2-15pm from Liverpool Exchange to Glasgow Central, with its portions from Manchester Victoria and for Edinburgh Princes Street, passes Morecambe South Junction's Down home signal. Note the Fogman's hut to the south of the junction signals.

Hest Bank

PEJ746
23rd March 1957
An easterly wind blows towards Morecambe Bay as ex-LNWR G2a 0-8-0 49144 from Springs Branch shed heads south from Hest Bank with the 10-35am Class J empty wagons train from Carnforth to Ince Moss, south of Wigan. The single line to Bare Lane has left the main line by this point, running behind the permanent way cabin.

PEC092
22nd September 1951
An animated scene at Hest Bank as spotters of all ages record ex-LMS 7P *Royal Scot* 4-6-0 46110 *Grenadier Guardsman* rolling through with train W508, a Whitley Bay to Morecambe excursion. The tender behind Upperby's 46110 is still in LMS livery well over three years after Nationalisation and its train appears to be made up entirely of ex-LNER Gresley-designed stock. Note how the Down Starter colour-light signal has been located on the footbridge.

PEF998
22nd April 1955
An unusual sight at Hest Bank on a Friday lunchtime: Fell diesel 2B+B2 10100 heads north with a mobile test train. The loco was originally built as a 2D2 (4-8-4) by a joint venture of Fell Developments Ltd – owners of transmission design – Messrs Ricardo & Co and the Railway Executive. It was built at Derby to the design of HG Ivatt and ran for several years on trains between St Pancras and Manchester Central before suffering a major failure. It became BR property and was repaired in 1955, when it received the then BR diesel green livery. This photograph must have been taken soon after it came out of the works and it is seen heading to Carlisle, Kingmoor shed, for tests on the Settle to Carlisle line. It had left Derby that morning for Crewe North shed, where it had picked up its test train of three mobile test units, a dynamometer car and a mobile workshop. Ex-Lancashire & Yorkshire Railway dynamometer car 45050 can be seen immediately behind the loco.

PEK348
20th July 1958
Brighton-built diesel 1-Co-Co-1 10203 runs wrong line through Hest Bank with train W136, the Up *Royal Scot*. Unlike the other pioneer main line diesels, 10203 had a 2000hp engine and has been deemed capable of handling the twelve-carriage train single handed. The loco certainly looks smart in its lined green livery. As ever at Hest Bank, the passing train has caught the attention of the holidaymakers and spotters on the footbridge.

Hest Bank

PES263
20th May 1961
Taking water at speed: ex-LMS 7P *Rebuilt Scot* 4-6-0 46105 *Cameron Highlander* with the 4-30pm from Glasgow Central to Manchester, train W140, with its through portions from Edinburgh Waverley and for Liverpool Exchange. The Polmadie loco is taking water on Hest Bank troughs. The troughs and surrounding track are in excellent condition with timbers and setts providing drainage and protecting the track from waste water. It is hoped that the fireman will raise the scoop as soon as the tender is full and before water overflows down the sides of the leading carriages!

PEJ832
15th June 1957
LMS 8P *Princess Royal* 4-6-2 46206 *Princess Marie Louise* passes over Hest Bank troughs with train W126, the Up *Mid-Day Scot*, and is about to pass through the station. This Limited Load train was given five minutes between Carnforth and Lancaster Castle on its non-stop run from Carlisle to Crewe. Most of the carriages carry the latest BR livery.

PEJ833
15th June 1957
LMS 8P *Princess Coronation* 4-6-2 46226 *Duchess of Norfolk* with the 12-02pm from Perth to Euston, train W484. The fireman on 46226 will be about to raise the scoop after taking water. This Limited Load train was scheduled to pass Carnforth at 5-09pm with arrival at Lancaster Castle at 5-15pm. Bolton-le-Sands village is in right background.

PEJ837
15th June 1957
It is 6 o'clock on a bright evening as ex-LMS 6P *Jubilee* 4-6-0 45661 *Vernon* takes water on Hest Bank troughs. This is the 4-15pm from Manchester Victoria to Glasgow Central, train W282. If the tender is full then our photographer may be in for an unexpected soaking.

PEK737
5th August 1959
Ex-LMS 8P *Princess Coronation* 4-6-2 46249 *City of Sheffield* and the Down *Mid-Day Scot* rushes over Hest Bank troughs without taking water. If she is on time, the *Mid-Day Scot* will have passed through Lancaster at 5-45pm and will be passing Carnforth at 5-50pm.

PEK740
5th August 1959
BR 7MT *Britannia* 4-6-2 70050, *Firth of Clyde* cruises over Hest Bank troughs with its tender overflowing, after taking water. Hopefully the guard will have walked down the train after leaving Lancaster to check that carriage windows are closed. This is Train C402, the 4-15pm from Manchester Victoria and 4-25pm from Liverpool Exchange for Glasgow Central with a portion for Edinburgh Princes Street.

Bolton-le-Sands

PEK301
27th May 1958
Ex-LMS 5MT 4-6-0 45326 passes under Pasture Lane with the 9-50am from Manchester Victoria to Workington Main via Bolton Trinity Street, train C388.

PEK373
24th July 1958
Ex-LMS 6P *Patriot* 4-6-0 45503 *The Royal Leicestershire Regiment* passes Milepost 4 with the 4-10pm from Carlisle to Manchester Victoria. Train W128 will have left Carnforth at 5-51pm for its nine minute run to Lancaster. Bolton-le-Sands is in the background.

PEZ237
11th August 1964
It is almost 8pm on a bright summer evening as ex-LMS 4F 0-6-0 44386 saunters towards Bolton-le-Sands with the evening Class K goods from Heysham to Carnforth. 44386 carries an electrification stripe on cab side, indicating it is not allowed to work south of Crewe under the then new 25kv overhead electrification wires. Four years later, this will be the last scheduled steam train to be worked by Carnforth shed, on 3rd August 1968 although 44386 will only last a further nine months in service.

PEK374
24th July 1958
Ex-LMS 6P *Jubilee* 4-6-0 45655 *Keith* with the 3-55pm Manchester Exchange to Barrow Central, via Tyldesley and Wigan North Western. Seen approaching Bolton-le-Sands on a beautiful summer's evening with a breeze blowing off Morecambe Bay, train W37 will have left Hest Bank at about 5-53pm and not stop until Carnforth.

Bolton-le-Sands

PEK196
6th April 1958

It is about 3-15pm on a cloudy Sunday afternoon and relaying work is underway near Pasture Lane, to the south of Bolton-le-Sands. Ex-LMS 6P *Jubilee* 4-6-0 45558 *Manitoba* pilots ex-LMS 7P *Rebuilt Scot* 4-6-0 46104 *Scottish Borderer* on train W28, the 10-40am from Glasgow Central to Manchester Victoria, with portions from Edinburgh Princes Street and for Liverpool Exchange. Despite the closeness of the passing train, the track gang finds no need to leave the "four foot". This is a heavy train of 15 assorted Mark 1 and LMS-design carriages.

PEK378
24th July 1958
LMS-design 4MT 2-6-4T 42136 accelerates away from Bolton-le-Sands station with the 5-05pm
from Lakeside to Morecambe Promenade before coasting to its next stop at Hest Bank. A mix
of LMS-design stock in both old and new British Railways liveries make up this popular summer
seasonal working.

PEK299
27th May 1958
The 7-15am goods from Whitehaven Corkickle to St. Helens is running under Class D headlamps, indicating it can run at
express goods speeds, having at least 30% of its vans XP rated. The train, behind ex-LMS 5MT 4-6-0 44936, is approaching
Pasture Lane at around 11-30am.

Bolton-le-Sands

PEK376
24th July 1958
Ex-LMS 3F 0-6-0T 47339 has just passed through Bolton-le-Sands with the 6-10pm goods from Carnforth to Lancaster. Although only a class K goods train, it will have to be punctual as train W126, the 3-00pm from Glasgow Central to Euston, the 4-40pm Carlisle to Broad St Goods and the Lakeside to Morecambe train will be close behind in short succession!

PEK377
24th July 1958
Ex-LMS 5MT 4-6-0 45412 heads south of Bolton-le-Sands with the 4-40pm Carlisle to London, Broad Street express goods. Running as a Class C Parcels, Fish, Livestock, Milk, Fruit or Perishables, all XP stock train, this train will take about 10 minutes from Carnforth to Lancaster, as good a speed as any Class B passenger train yet showing little sign of effort on this warm clear evening.

PEK209
9th April 1958
Train W67, behind ex-LMS 8P *Princess Royal* 4-6-2 46206 *Princess Marie Louise,* approaches Dertern Yeat. This is the 11-25am from Birmingham New Street to Glasgow Central. The bungalows at left under construction are on St Nicholas Road with Merefell Road, behind: the beginning of the infilling of the fields between the A6 and railway north of Bolton-le-Sands. Mill Lane passes over the bridge in the background, with Bolton-le-Sands station beyond

PEQ053
17th May 1951
Looking quite smart in its lined black passenger livery, ex-LMS 3MT 2-6-2T 40041 trundles south of Bolton-le-Sands with the 6-10pm goods from Carnforth to Lancaster. The train is running under Class J headlamps, nominally for through mineral or empty wagons trains but in this case indicating a slow goods. St Mary and the Angels Roman Catholic church can be seen in the distance.

PEF549
3rd April 1953
Bolton-le-Sands was one of the original stations on the Lancaster & Carlisle Railway and retained low platforms until closure from 3rd February 1969. Despite being on the West Coast main line, its level crossing was worked by station staff, its signalbox having been closed in the 1880s although not removed until around 1910. From then the crossing had only been protected by Distant signals worked from the platform but in May 1937 the LMS installed intermediate block signals, also acting to protect the crossing. These LMS single lens "searchlight" signals can be seen either side of the footbridge.

PEJ749
22nd March 1957
Ex-LMS 5MT 4-6-0 44892 heads south towards Dertern Yeat (or Gate) and Bolton-le-Sands with the 1-35pm from Barrow Central to Preston. It is about a quarter-mile south of the three sets of Travelling Post Office lineside equipment on the Up side with their attendant white painted huts. Up on the hillside at right can be seen Barker's Bridge on the Lancaster Canal and the A6 just below it, busy for a spring Sunday afternoon.

Lancaster, Ovangle Bridge,

PEB674
Undated, possibly August Bank Holiday 1953
British Railways locomotives looked very smart when painted in the lined passenger black livery as seen here. The 3-05pm from Morecambe Promenade to Lancaster Castle is seen here with ex-LMS 2P 0-4-4T 41903 propelling a three carriage pull & push set away from Ovangle Bridge with Scale Hall farm at left. The different types of catenary and masts make an interesting contrast to what is otherwise a typical 1950s steam railway.

Four - The Midland Railway:
- from Lancaster to the Sea

THE COVERAGE of the old North Western Railway and Midland lines has been split into several chapters: the steam services west of Lancaster, the "Little North Western" lines east of Lancaster, and the Lancaster Morecambe and Heysham electric trains.

The Morecambe Harbour and Railway Company was the originator of the line from Green Ayre to its harbour at Poulton (which would rename itself Morecambe after the adjacent bay) but soon lost its identity after merger with the North Western Railway. The harbour became a port for Ireland, developed somewhat by the Midland, although the Derby company moved its main Irish Sea fleet to the Furness Railway's deep water pier at Piel in 1867, and in 1882 to the FR Ramsden Dock

facility. Irish Sea traffic returned to the southern side of Morecambe Bay in 1904 with the opening of Heysham Harbour. Whilst the Morecambe company had but a short life, its railway line was to last 120 years.

The Midland line through Lancaster may have lacked the glamour of the main line expresses on the Lancaster & Carlisle section through Castle station but it could offer the variety of trains expected on a secondary main line to the seaside, especially during the summer when excursionists from West Yorkshire travelled in their thousands to the bracing delights of Morecambe. Express goods trains were also the order of the day, taking cargoes to and from Northern Ireland via Heysham harbour.

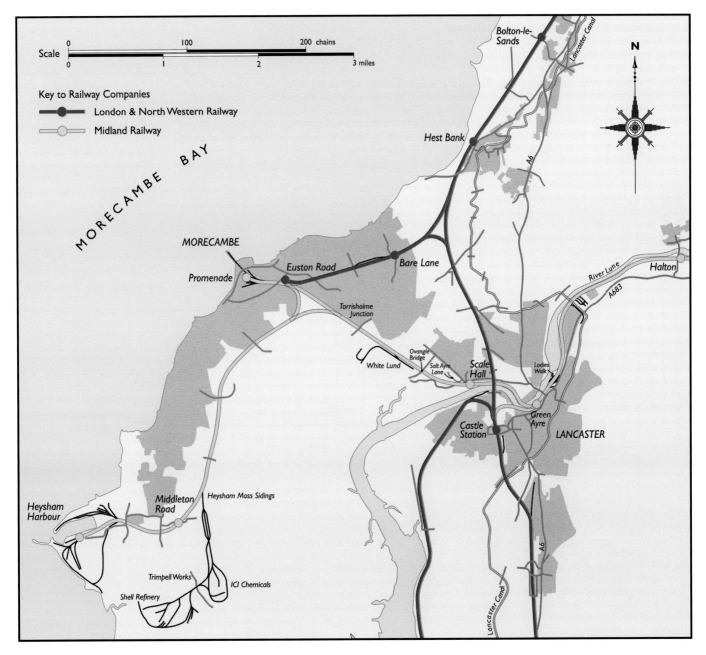

Lancaster Ladies Walk

PEO013
2nd September 1950
An excursion from Leeds City (North) and Bradford Forster Square to Morecambe Promenade approaches Ladies Walk signal box. The ex-Midland 4P Compound 4-4-0 41005, from Green Ayre shed, is showing a clear exhaust as it passes the Standfast works. The first of the non-corridor carriages is annotated Local Set 163. Surprisingly for a Saturday, the train is not carrying a reporting number.

Lancaster New Zealand Sidings

PES242
3rd April 1961
An Easter Monday excursion hauled by ex-LMS 5MT 4-6-0 44828 approaches Skerton Bridge. The train is N571 from Leeds to Morecambe Promenade and appears to be made up of mainly ex-LNER stock painted maroon with the odd carriage still in crimson and cream. The first two vehicles are a Gresley Tourist Third Open articulated pair. This is the eastern limit of the Lancaster-Morecambe-Heysham electrification with the easternmost masts at left and behind the train. New Zealand sidings are to the right with Ladies Walk sidings to the left behind the train, both full to capacity.

Lancaster Green Ayre

PEJ802
10th June 1957
The safety valves are blowing as ex-LMS 5MT 4-6-0 45330 enters Green Ayre station with a Down excursion. Unfortunately the usually meticulous Pearsalls have not noted anything about this train. It could be that train C925, from the London Midland Region Central lines, is from East Lancashire, joining the North Western line at Hellifield.

PEK953
18th April 1960
Passengers waiting for the next train to Leeds and Bradford watch ex-LNER B1 4-6-0 61020 and train N970, an Easter Monday Leeds to Morecambe Promenade excursion, as it rolls into Green Ayre station past the LMS-built signalbox of 1932. The train appears to consist of mainly ex-LNER Gresley stock of various types all in the current maroon livery. The gradients on the track here are emphasized and show how the railway was built to dip under the road level of Thomas Harrison's Skerton Bridge of 1788.

PEK197
5th or 7th April 1958
It is probably Easter Saturday or Easter Monday as Morecambe-bound excursion N972 rolls through Green Ayre and over the junction with the branch to Castle station. Ex-LNER J39/1 0-6-0 64754 is from Ardsley shed and its LMS-design stock is still in the old crimson and cream livery. The new road roller will wait until the next working day to be unloaded from the lowmac wagon in the carriage dock.

Lancaster Green Ayre

PEF935
1st November 1954

Ex-LMS 3F 0-6-0T 47471 works hard as it enters Green Ayre station with the 2-30pm trip working from New Zealand sidings to Castle station goods yard. Ahead of the Class K branch goods lays the half-mile climb at 1 in 78 to Castle station; the crew will be hoping for a clear run to bring their train onto the level tracks through the platforms at Lancaster Castle without stopping.

Lancaster Castle

PED091
10th March 1950

Steam escapes from beneath ex-MR 3F 0-6-0 43187 as it stalls attempting to bring its train off the 1 in 78 gradient and onto level track through Castle station. This trip working of former Private Owner wagons from New Zealand sidings is running as a Class J train. Someone has made an attempt to repaint, or at least clean, the smokebox of 43187, presumably as a start to applying British Railways livery. Despite its carrying a BR number plate, its cab side still displays LMS-style numerals and the tender retains LMS livery. Although built in 1887, 43187 has another ten years of useful life ahead of it.

PEB142
2nd January 1953

Between 12th February 1951 and 17th August 1953 British Railways re-equipped the old Midland Railway electrical equipment between Lancaster, Morecambe and Heysham. Steam motor or "Push & Pull" sets replaced the old electric motor cars during this period with ex-LMS Stanier 2P 0-4-4 tank engines providing the motive power. Numbers 41900 and 41902– 41904 were transferred from Bath Green Park to join 41901 at Green Ayre shed. Here 2P 0-4-4T 41903 propels its 'Push & Pull' set out of Castle station towards Green Ayre with the 2-18pm to Morecambe Promenade.

Scale Hall

PEJ796
8th June 1957

Opening day for a new station. Ex-LMS 4P Compound 4-4-0 41186 runs through the brand new station at Scale Hall with the 4-55pm Saturdays Only train from Leeds City (North) to Morecambe Promenade. On the Down platform ten of the estimated 1,400 passengers from that first day await the next electric train for Morecambe.

PEJ795
8th June 1957

Looking east from the Morecambe end of the Down platform towards Carlisle Bridge. Work is not quite finished at the new station: temporary electric lighting has been provided on both platforms and cabling is awaiting fixture of permanent lamps. Markers in some windows of the Up platform building show that glazing is recent.

Ovangle Bridge

PEB223
probably 27th March 1953

Ivatt 4MT 2-6-0 43034 storms under Ovangle Road bridge with a Class D express goods heading towards Lancaster. This is the western end of the "Golden Mile" of experimental catenary; Midland design gantries with their wooden poles are beyond the bridge whilst the nearest mast is reminiscent of the type used twenty years later when the London Midland Region extended its West Coast Main Line electrification from Weaver Junction to Glasgow.

Morecambe White Lund

PEZ773
15th August 1966
Ex-LMS 5MT 4-6-0 44912 passes White Lund sidings with the 2-50pm Class C fully fitted express goods from Heysham to Stourton. In the six months since closure to passengers, the old catenary has been de-wired but the old MR portals still stand. White Lund sidings to the left have served the White Lund Gas Works since 1959. Gas production will only last around 20 years in total, with rail service lasting until the end of January 1970 (the official closure with effect from 2nd February). Gas production will cease with the coming of North Sea gas. After closure of the line from Morecambe to Lancaster in 1967, White Lund will be reached by a siding from Torrisholme No 2 junction. Intriguingly the ground frame at Torrisholme No 2 will remain for another year, suggesting some infrequent use of the siding. Just yards east of the section controlled by Torrisholme No 1 signal box, White Lund ground frame is released from Green Ayre signal box, two miles to the east, until closure of that stretch of line.

PEF987
9th April 1955
Ex-Midland Railway 4F 0-6-0 44007 rumbles past White Lund with a morning Class D express goods for Stourton. The train is made up largely of fitted box vans and containers loaded on a variety of 1, 3 and 6 plank open wagons. The disused siding in the foreground once served the erstwhile White Lund Tarmac works, itself situated on a Great War munitions factory site. The building in the left background is Pickford's storage depot and formerly part of the munitions factory. Within five years this location will be busy again, when White Lund Gasworks and new rail sidings are built nearby.

Torrisholme

PEZ995
3rd June 1967
The last through train from Heysham via Lancaster Green Ayre to the West Riding passes Torrisholme No 1 signal box. This is the 3-05pm Class C goods from Heysham Moss Sidings via Morecambe Promenade goods yard to Leeds, Neville Hill, and hauled by ex-LMS 5MT 4-6-0 44898. After this train, the sections from Morecambe (the junction with the line to Bare Lane) to Torrisholme No 1 Junction, White Lund sidings to Lancaster Green Ayre and Lancaster power station to Wennington will see no more scheduled trains, with signal boxes along the line being closed with effect from Monday 5th June 1967.

PEF926
25th September 1954
Ardsley shed have turned out an immaculate ex-LNER B1 4-6-0 61131 for this Wakefield to Morecambe Promenade excursion. Train 990 is approaching Torrisholme No 1 signal box. Despite the cloudy skies, 61131 has a clear exhaust and steam to spare. The carriages include former LNER designs, the first and third being Gresley design (the third still in teak finish) while the second and fourth are Thompson designs. The suburbs of Morecambe are extending towards Lancaster including the row of houses being built on Christie Avenue.

PEB214
Possibly March 1953
Ex-LMS 3F 0-6-0T 47381 from Green Ayre shed trundles towards Torrisholme No. 1 Junction with a Down Class K branch goods train. Intriguingly, this consists of a pair of non-corridor carriages sandwiched between pairs of mineral wagons.

White Lund

PEJ558
25th August 1956

Ex-LMS 4P Compound 4-4-0 41180 rushes past the site of the erstwhile White Lund munitions factory with a Leeds City (North) to Morecambe Promenade train. From 1916 the site was occupied by National Filling Factory No 13, served by its own platforms for the 3000 men and women working here. Here shells from the National Projectile Factory in Lancaster, also adjacent to the Midland line, and the Vickers, Sons & Maxim works at Barrow were filled. Both factories were run by Vickers as part of the war effort. On the night of 1st October 1917 an unexplained fire led to three days of fire and exploding shells which rocked Lancaster and Morecambe and were heard as far away as Burnley.

Scola Green Lane Crossing

PEO027
9th September 1950

Ivatt 4MT 2-6-0 43035 accelerates away from Morecambe Promenade with the 11-20am train to Leeds City (North). Although the loco is only just over a year old, the train is made up entirely of old wooden non-corridor stock, not pleasant for a journey of perhaps three hours but typical of the period. The line to Heysham is curving away at left while the carriages at right are actually in platform 5 at Euston Road station. The impact and simplicity of the Midland's wooden catenary portals, even at a junction, are shown to good effect here.

Morecambe Promenade

PEJ554
25th August 1955

With a good head of steam, ex-LMS 5MT *Crab* 2-6-0 42928 pulls out of platform 1 at Morecambe Promenade with an unidentified train of assorted non-corridor stock. Meanwhile in platform 2, an unidentified 4P Compound 4-4-0 has backed onto a recent arrival; holidaymakers are leaving the train and walking along the platform with their suitcases. A rake of ex-LMS corridor stock waits for its return excursion in the sidings at the entrance to the goods yard. Within the confines of Promenade station, the Midland placed more substantial steel lattice gantries for its electrification project instead of the simple timber portals.

A67-29-1
5th August 1967
With only three months service left, ex-LMS 5MT 4-6-0 44964 passes Heysham Station signal box as it approaches Heysham station. Despite running tender first, the train is running with an express headcode. It will have reversed at Morecambe Promenade, all access to Morecambe and Heysham now being via the ex-LNWR branch whether from Lancaster Castle and the south or from former Midland territory via Carnforth. This will later form special train 1T50, departing at 6-28pm for Liverpool Exchange.

PE1699
12th July 1969
The 18-10 to Manchester Victoria pulls away from Heysham Harbour station, crossing from Platform 3 to the Up Passenger line for Morecambe. BR English Electric Type 4 D231 *Sylvania* has lost at least one of her nameplates by the time of this photograph. For six weekends during the summer, BR ran a daytime sailing to Belfast and return. This is one of the connecting trains, the others running to Leeds City and Birmingham New Street.

Lancaster, Carlisle Bridge

PEJ402
1st April 1956

The 5-55pm Lancaster Castle to Morecambe Promenade is strengthened to two units for the Easter Day service. The train includes Motor Open Brake Thirds M28221M and M28219M (the units would be reclassified as second class as with all third class stock on BR as of 3rd June that year). The unit is running along the north bank of the Lune, at the eastern end of the experimental catenary, with Carlisle Bridge of the former LNWR main line and St Georges Quay beyond. The Ashton memorial stands on the skyline, overlooking the city from Williamson Park.

Five - The Morecambe Electrics

THE STORY of the electric trains on the Lancaster-Morecambe-Heysham route is well documented, both as a pioneering experiment of 1908 for the possible electrification of the Midland Railway's London suburban services and main line through the High Peak, and again in the early 1950s as an experiment for main line electrification of British Railways. As a compact service it needed few units both in its original guise and after the line was re-equipped. The old Midland men must have been upset though, with the "new" trains being rebuilds of former LNWR stock almost as old as the cars they replaced.

Following training of the motor-men, the electric service was reintroduced on 17th August 1953. The mayors of Lancaster, Morecambe and Heysham were treated to a ride on the first train. At the celebratory luncheon their hosts, British Railways, announced that a recommendation had been put to the British Transport Commission for a new halt between Lancaster and Morecambe. Scale Hall station was opened on 8th June 1957 to serve the nearby housing estates. Unfortunately with the impact of the Beeching Report, Scale Hall would only stay open for an all too brief eight and a half years, closing with the withdrawal of the electric service and the direct trains from Morecambe, via Green Ayre, to Yorkshire.

All was not plain sailing for the newly re-introduced electric trains. The opening of the Holme Moss television transmitter on 12th October 1951 allowed the people of Lancaster, Morecambe and Heysham to receive a clear BBC Television signal for the first time. The Coronation in June 1953 had led to more families investing in televisions, including some living close to the railway. These television owners, no doubt proud of the expensive but sensitive new sets, were suddenly aware of the frequency of the new service. Every passing train caused interference (although it's possible every passing car or lorry did too). The Post Office were called in to investigate and in early December 1953, for around a week, off peak services had to revert to steam whilst the engineers worked on the problem.

As mentioned in the captions, a section of the line on the north bank of the Lune between Carlisle Bridge, where the line passed under the Lancaster & Carlisle main line, and Ovangle Bridge, two thirds of a mile to the west, was the site of a further experiment. This time British Insulated Callander's Cables were allowed to replace the old Midland timber catenary portals with their latest designs in variety, both for testing and for demonstration to prospective buyers. This was the "Golden Mile".

Now this section is largely cycle and footpaths, where the inquisitive can still find the odd base of a catenary mast and notice the rise in the land where Scale Hall station platforms once stood.

ENGLAND'S LATEST SEASIDE HOTEL

MIDLAND HOTEL MORECAMBE

The importance of Morecambe to the LMS was confirmed when in 1933 it opened the art deco Midland Hotel, which stayed in railway ownership until 1952 and remains as an icon on the town's promenade.

Image: National Railway Museum/Science & Society Library

Lancaster, Green Ayre

PEJ801
10th June 1957
A special working led by Motor Open Brake Second M28220M enters the Down platform at Green Ayre station, having crossed from the Up line by the crossing just beyond Skerton Bridge (the limit of electrification). The guard or driver has yet to cover the red tail lamp and uncover one of the electric headlamps or - as was often the case - fix an oil lamp at the head of the train.

PEO066
26th December 1950
Former Midland Railway motor car 28610 leads driving trailer M22202M into Promenade station with a train from Lancaster. Although the LMS had ceased to exist almost three years previously, the motor car still retains its LMS red livery. It will be withdrawn six weeks later on 12th February 1951 prior to the re-equipping of the Lancaster-Morecambe-Heysham electrified railway.

Lancaster, Ovangle Bridge

PEB225
27th March 1953

A newly re-equipped ex-LNWR EMU with Motor Open Brake Third M28221M leading heads towards Ovangle Bridge on a test train to Morecambe Promenade. At this stage the units were undergoing trials and being used for driver training. Three types of catenary mast are visible here, at the western end of the "Golden Mile". The quayside buildings of Lancaster can be seen in the background. An Asda supermarket car park now occupies the field to the right whilst a housing estate has been built on the fields of Scale Hall Farm at left.

Torrisholme

PEB217
25th March 1953
One of the ex-LNWR EMUs with unidentified Driving Trailer Open Third leading and Motor Open Brake Third M28219M at the rear of a three-car train crossing over Torrisholme No 1 Junction for Morecambe Promenade. This must be a driver-training run or a test train since the public electric train service wouldn't re-commence for another five months. Although the electrical equipment and wiring are brand new, the EMU was built in 1914 for the LNWR and re-equipped for use here while the masts and gantry are original Midland Railway structures from 1908. To aid identification, the driving units will later have their car numbers painted on the unit ends. The spread of suburban Morecambe is evidenced by the housing under construction at left.

PEF925
25th September 1954
Apart from the upper quadrant signals, this view to the west at Torrisholme No 1 Junction is pure Midland Railway. The track ahead leads to Morecambe Promenade with the line to Heysham Harbour going off to the left. The simplicity of the electrical equipment supported on wooden poles, with the wrought iron gantry for carrying the wires over three or more tracks, is most attractive.

Salt Ayre Lane

PEB110
Undated

Detail of one of the experimental masts and catenary near the bridge over Salt Ayre Lane, looking towards Ovangle Bridge. Scale Hall station will be built behind the photographer.

PEF977
13th March 1955

Rebuilding the bridge over Salt Ayre Lane. Here a road crane removes the centre girder whilst baulks, rails and other components of the bridge litter the roadside, watched by as many 'trilby hats and overcoats' as workmen. To allow the crane's jib to get between them, the overhead wires have been pulled aside by simply dropping or swinging around the catenary, a feature of the modern masts not possible on the earlier Midland Railway portals. The two rail mounted hand cranes appear not to be needed for this part of the proceedings. On the far side of the bridge a local couple seem intrigued by the work.

Halton

PEJ341
12th November 1955
63 year-old ex-MR 2P 4-4-0 40409 leads the younger ex-LMS 4P Compound 4-4-0 41045 away from Halton with the 2-46pm train from Morecambe Promenade to Leeds City (North). Trees hide the mills and village of Halton on the north bank of the river Lune, while the low November sun casts long shadows across the scene.

Six - The Midland Railway: To the Dales

A SHORT excursion beyond Lancaster along the old North Western Railway and back to Carnforth on the Furness & Midland. In LMS and BR days, passenger trains from Leeds and Bradford would split at Wennington with the main train heading for Morecambe whilst two or three carriages would be worked to Carnforth.

Wennington was one of those places worth visiting until the closure of the old North Western Railway line on to Morecambe in 1966, for here trains regularly combined or split. First to arrive would be the train from Carnforth with passengers for Bradford and Leeds. After briefly doing business in the main line platform, the train would be drawn forward and shunted into the bay platform, which faced the Skipton direction. The loco would then uncouple and move onto the westbound lines and run forward onto the old Furness & Midland Joint line, beyond the signal box and junction. The train from Morecambe Promenade or Lancaster Green Ayre would then arrive; do whatever business it had in the main line platform and also draw forward before reversing to couple onto the carriages in the bay platform. It would depart for Skipton with the train being split later in its journey, with some carriages for Leeds City

(North) and others for Bradford Forster Square. A train from Leeds and Bradford would arrive soon afterwards and be split. The train engine would leave with the Lancaster and Morecambe portion, leaving the Carnforth portion in the westbound platform. The Carnforth loco would then draw back from beyond the junction to couple up and depart for Carnforth.

Stations along both lines closed west of Wennington in the 50s and 60s. By the time passenger services ceased between Wennington and Morecambe via Lancaster Green Ayre on 3rd January 1966, only Halton remained to the east of Lancaster. Goods trains were diverted via Carnforth about 18 months later to allow the line to be closed between Wennington and Morecambe Promenade on 4th June 1967. The section from Lancaster Castle to Lancaster Power Station remained open until 16th March 1976 and from Torrisholme No 2 Box to White Lund gas works until 2nd February 1970.

Today the NWR east of Lancaster over the Crook o'Lune viaducts is part of a cycleway whilst the few daily Leeds – Lancaster – Morecambe trains continue to pass over the Furness & Midland.

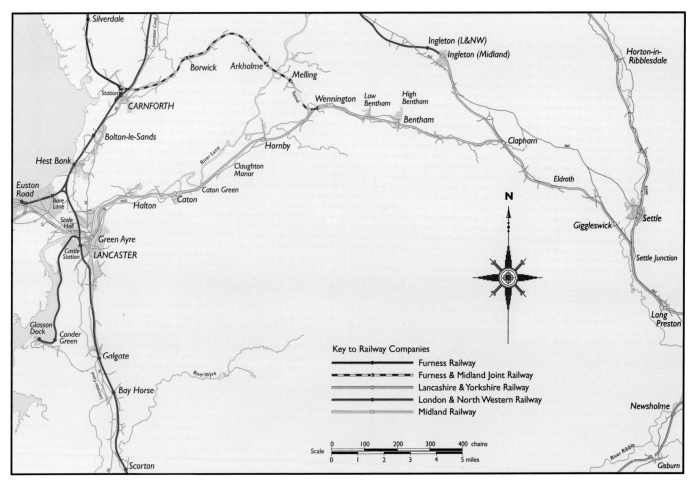

Key to Railway Companies
- Furness Railway
- Furness & Midland Joint Railway
- Lancashire & Yorkshire Railway
- London & North Western Railway
- Midland Railway

Halton

PEJ811
11th June 1957
Ex-LMS 6P *Patriot* 4-6-0 45542 passes through Halton station in fine form with train M568, the 2-25pm from Morecambe Promenade to Bradford Forster Square. Being Whit Bank Holiday Monday, the train is strengthened to eleven carriages.

Crook o' Lune

PEF411
13th September 1952
61 year-old ex-MR 3F 0-6-0 43293 has just passed over the western Lune viaduct at Crook o' Lune with a Class K pickup goods on its return from Clapham to Lancaster. Green Ayre shed will continue to use this veteran for another 15 months. Caton Up Distant is in the background.

PEF406
13th September 1952
Crook o' Lune, to the west of Caton, has been a local
beauty spot for several centuries with its loop in the
river Lune and view to the northwest up the Lune
valley. The North Western Railway chose a route
involving two attractive viaducts to cross the bends
in the river. Here Ivatt 4MT 2-6-0 43113 of Skipton
shed crosses the western viaduct with the 2-10pm
from Morecambe Promenade to Leeds, recorded
as an excursion train, made up of early period LMS
carriages.

Caton

PEF412
21st December 1952
Ex-LMS 4P Compound 4-4-0 41196 rounds the curve
from Caton towards the Crook o' Lune east viaduct
with a train for Morecambe Promenade. The house
on the right is now named Glenogle and stands just
beyond Mill Lane.

Caton

PEF930
2nd October 1954
Running through Caton with a clear exhaust is ex-LMS 5MT *Crab* 2-6-0 42771 and train M541, an excursion from Leeds City (North) and Bradford Forster Square to Morecambe Promenade. Typical of the day, the train is made up of non-corridor stock; no doubt the excursionists will be making a dash for the commodious lavatories on arrival at Promenade station! Caton would close entirely on 1st May 1961 despite the village having several significant industries.

Caton Green

A64-03-2
30th March 1964
BR Sulzer Type 2, D7568, approaches with train 2M73, the 8-30am from Bradford Forster Square to Morecambe Promenade. Despite being in service for only six months, the loco has become very grubby. Its train will have dropped off through carriages for Carnforth at Wennington. The Up Distant signal is for Lane Foot Crossing. From the beginning of March this class of diesel loco (together with the larger BR Sulzer Type 4 *Peaks*) had taken over most remaining steam-hauled trains on this service, with other Leeds/Bradford – Morecambe services handled by diesel multiple units.

Claughton Manor

PEF958
18th January 1955
Brighton-built ex-LMS 8F 2-8-0 48616 has had a small snow plough fitted for the wintery weather and is hauling a Down goods train past the Claughton Brick & Tile Company's siding. The train is running with a Class J through mineral head code, suggesting that its crew are in no rush to get to Lancaster.

Caton Green

PE1335
possibly May 1965

On a misty grey day, ex-LMS 5MT 4-6-0 44886 runs alongside the Lune with the 2-55pm express goods from Heysham to Stourton. XP rated vans and container wagons make up this Class C train, the containers being shipped through from Belfast on that morning's ferry. The ex-MR Up Distant on the right is for Lane Foot level crossing.

Claughton Manor

PEF959
18th January 1955

The Lune valley is covered in snow as ex-LMS 8F 2-8-0 48105 rumbles eastwards with an Up Class H train of empty wagons. The rear of the train is passing over Lane Foot Crossing between Caton and Claughton Manor.

Wennington

PEJ172
6th July 1955
A busy scene at Wennington with ex-LMS 4F 0-6-0 44479 of Lower Darwen shed rolling through on a Down mineral train, signalled for the Lancaster line. Meanwhile, the 6-58pm from Morecambe Promenade to Leeds City (North) is shunted back to pick up the 7-00pm through carriages from Carnforth. The railwaymen are preparing to couple the two portions, the Carnforth carriages standing out of sight to their left. Note that the rear carriage on the Morecambe portion of the train is in crimson livery indicating a non-corridor carriage. The passengers from Carnforth would thus be isolated from the rest of the train.

PEJ894
24th August 1957
Ex-LMS 4P Compound 4-4-0 41060 approaches Wennington with the 10-45am Saturdays Only train from Leeds City (North) to Carnforth. The track to the right is the longer of two Down lie-by sidings which in LMS days became a loop from the Down line.

PEJ720
27th January 1957
After arrival at Wennington, the 2-43pm from Carnforth is set back into bay by its train engine, ex-LMS
3MT 2-6-2T 40011, to await the arrival of the 2-46pm from Morecambe Promenade.

PEJ722
27th January 1957
Veteran ex-MR 2P 4-4-0 40409
and ex-LMS 4P Compound
4-4-0 41152 produce lots
of steam as they get away
from Wennington with the
combined 2-43pm from
Carnforth / 2-46pm from
Morecambe Promenade
to Leeds City (North) and
Bradford Forster Square,
the train from Morecambe
having collected the Carnforth
portion from the bay.

Low Bentham

PEK225
12th April 1958
Having picked up its through carriages from Carnforth, ex-LMS 5MT 4-6-0 44900 steams along the Wenning valley with the 4-20pm from Morecambe Promenade to Leeds City (North) and Bradford Forster Square. The skies are heavy and the weather still cold after threatened snow on the previous weekend, Easter; 44900 still carries a small snowplough. The train is approaching Low Bentham from Wennington; Wennington Down Distant signal is in the distance.

PEK226
12th April 1958
Heading west from Low Bentham under leaden skies, BR 5MT 4-6-0 73010 heads the 3-12pm from Leeds City (North) to Morecambe Promenade past the rear of Holmes toll house. At Wennington the rear two or three carriages will be detached, to be taken forward to Carnforth.

Bentham

PEJ499
11th July 1956
69 year-old ex-MR 3F 0-6-0 43178 heads eastwards from Bentham with the 12-40pm Class H through goods train from Carnforth to Skipton. The train behind the loco is made up of both wooden and steel bodied empty mineral wagons, possibly from Roosecote Power Station at Barrow-in-Furness. The ex-MR Distant signal is for Bentham Station signal box and stands complete with its fogman's hut.

Ingleton

PEH739
22nd April 1962
Ingleton nestles alongside the river Greta, on the edge of the Pennines, and its railway viaduct fits very much into the scenery. In a classic view, BR Sulzer Type 4 D31 heads away from the former MR station and passes over the viaduct with the Down *Thames-Clyde Express*. The train has been diverted from the Settle – Carlisle section to run via Ingleton and Tebay. As it is Easter Sunday, this diversion is due to track maintenance rather than the more exciting blockage due to snow.

PEF778
7th January 1954
Ex-LMS 4F 0-6-0 44399 and the Clapham to Tebay goods waits patiently for the 2-09pm passenger train from Clapham to Lowgill to leave Ingleton station. The train is running with a Class J headcode although it is neither a through mineral train nor empty wagons. It is standing on the Down line with the brake van on Back Gate bridge. Ingleton signalbox not only controlled the small goods yard here, but also sidings serving the New Ingleton Colliery from 1913 to 1936. Once it has the road, 44399 will cross the viaduct and probably stop next at the former LNWR Thornton goods yard.

Clapham

PEH100
12th April 1958
The Bamber Bridge to Carlisle Class H through goods heads away from Clapham behind ex-LMS 5MT 2-6-0 42950. The main line to Lancaster and Morecambe is beyond the yard on the right; the farm curiously named Nutta is to the left.

PEJ205
1st August 1954
The 6-25pm return excursion from Ingleton to Leeds City (North) and Bradford Forster Square passes Clapham Up Outer Home signal. Train M543, hauled by ex-LMS 4F 0-6-0 44184, is approaching Nutta bridge at the west end of Clapham station. The hill in the right background is Grey Scars, on the edge of Ingleton Common. The size of the train shows the popularity of such excursions especially for ramblers in the 1950s.

Clapham

PED029
3rd September 1949
Ex-LMS 3MT 2-6-2T 40184 arrives at Clapham with a local passenger train from Low Gill. The main line curves away to the left, whilst the branch to Ingleton and Lowgill head straight on. This is a reminder of the North Western Railway's original ambition for its main line to pass through Ingleton and on to the LCR for Scotland. Circumstances dictated otherwise and the route to Lancaster and Morecambe became the main line, with the NWR and later Midland companies making do with a branch to Ingleton. After a false start the line from there to Lowgill was built by the LCR. It was only in LMS days that the route from Clapham to Lowgill was operated as a through line, although the level of traffic expected even then only required a train of a pair of non-corridor carriages.

PER101
undated, probably 1953
Clapham Junction, looking west towards Ingleton (ahead) and Lancaster (to left). An LMS-era Hawkseye sign has been taken off the wall in front of the station house whilst repainting is underway. A poster for the Coronation of the new Queen, located on the north side of the footbridge, gives a clue to the date of the photograph.

PEK223
12th April 1958
Ex-LMS 2P 4-4-0 40586 pilots an unidentified ex-LMS 4P Compound 4-4-0 away from Clapham with the 2-46pm train from Morecambe Promenade to Leeds City (North). Interestingly there is little coal in the tender of the leading loco suggesting it is returning to its home shed at Skipton; the seven LMS design corridor carriages would be a respectable load for a compound on this road. The rear two or three carriages are from Carnforth, having been attached to the train at Wennington.

Eldroth

PEJI15
April 1955

Ex-LMS 5MT 4-6-0 45293 passes Eldroth signal box and Down Home signal with a west-bound Class H through goods train bound for Heysham. Eldroth box broke the undulating five and a half mile section from Giggleswick to Clapham. The first and third wagons of the train look to be some form of insulated steel containers held in place with ropes attached to the container roofs.

Settle Junction

PEC080
20th September 1951
Looking towards Gigglewick with the Settle to Carlisle line climbing away steeply at a gradient of 1 in 102, ex-LMS 4P Compound 4-4-0 41196 approaches Settle Junction with a train from Morecambe Promenade for Leeds City (North). The train will include carriages from Carnforth, and for Bradford Forster Square.

PEC083
20th September 1951
Ivatt 2-6-0 43112 hauls the 5-00 pm goods from Giggleswick onto the main line at Settle Junction. The headcode indicates the train running as a Class H through goods or ballast train. Note how the track layout at the junction and associated signalling is influenced by the changes in gradient and the need for higher speeds on the Settle to Carlisle line. The tall Midland Railway Home signal above the loco is necessary if it is to be seen from beyond the overbridge by the crew of Up expresses, approaching from Carlisle at speed. Despite MR signals in use on this major route, this was, at the time, a very modern image scene with the Ivatt, based at Skipton, being only six months old.

Wennington

PEF580
21st April 1953

Blowing off steam, ex-LMS 4F 0-6-0 44467 of Stourton shed takes the Furness & Midland Joint line with the 5-00 pm goods train from Skipton to Carnforth, running under Class H through goods headlamps. Wennington signalbox is hidden by the junction signals, located to allow sighting by trains approaching through the station, beyond the overbridge. The train appears to be largely made up of former Private Owner wooden mineral wagons with a lone BR standard wagon. The loco tender has yet to receive its Lion and Wheel BR emblem.

Melling Tunnel

PEF579
21st April 1953

The 4-50pm through carriages from Carnforth for Leeds City (North) emerge from Melling tunnel behind BR Ivatt 4MT 2-6-0 43039 on the approach to Wennington. The train is passing the Distant signals for both Wennington and Melling. Once it has arrived at Wennington and any passengers have boarded or alighted, 43039 will shunt the three carriages into the bay platform to await the train from Morecambe Promenade. The mound high above the tunnel mouth is spoil, removed up the southerly of the four access shafts used in digging the tunnel.

Melling

PEF577
21st April 1953
The stations on the Furness & Midland Joint line combined mostly Midland Railway features such as layout and signalling equipment with station buildings that were not quite Furness Railway designs. Here is the easterly of the three stations on the F&M, Melling, looking towards Carnforth. Melling had closed to passenger traffic on 5th May 1952. Here we can see that the gas lamps on the platforms are being uprooted, many await collection, and other platform furniture has already been removed. Yet although the Midland signals are off and the signalbox is switched out, the goods yard is still open, and will remain so until 12th September 1960.

Arkholme

PEF574
21st April 1953
Unlike its neighbour, Melling, Arkholme is still open in this photograph, served by the Carnforth to Wennington service of through carriages to and from Leeds and Bradford. It will eventually close to all traffic on 12th September 1960, the general date of closure of local facilities on the F&M. In this mid-afternoon view looking towards Carnforth, the station is deserted, apart from a man walking through the empty goods yard. The station gardens are tidy, but await warmer spring weather before being planted. Perhaps the Furness Railway influenced its Midland partner to agree to such extravagant but handsome buildings for what were very local stations serving small, scattered communities often only a few miles from other stations.

Arkholme, Lune West Viaduct

PEF575
21st April 1953

Although just a mile apart, Melling and Arkholme stations were separated by the River Lune, on its journey south from the Pennines, east of Tebay, to Lancaster and Morecambe Bay. The Furness & Midland Joint line had two viaducts over the river, which for many years split into two for about half a mile exactly where it was crossed by the railway. The railway engineers had originally observed the main channel to pass under the eastern viaduct, but nature being her idiosyncratic self, its course shifted to the western viaduct. Here ex-LMS 5MT 4-6-0 45392 crosses the west viaduct as it coasts into Arkholme with the Carnforth through carriages from the 1-42pm from Leeds City (North) to Morecambe Promenade. A beautifully composed shot on a clear April day.

85

Bare Lane

PEJ183
26th July 1955

The Ulster Express approaches Bare Lane level crossing and station behind ex-LMS *Princess Coronation* 4-6-2 46257, *City of Salford*. Although giving a fine show, the driver has to limit his train to 30 mph on the Morecambe branch; a restriction only applied to Class 8P locomotives and the few large main line diesels. He will have to slow further to round the curve from Bare Lane to Morecambe South Junction at 25 mph and then 10 mph over the junction onto the main line. This train will have departed Heysham Harbour at 7-00 am. *City of Salford* will have been coupled onto Train W32 at Morecambe Promenade and will run non-stop to Crewe en route to Euston.

Seven - LNWR:
Branch Lines

WHILE THE Lancaster to Carlisle main line carried the glamorous trains and the Midland line had its compounds and visitors from the east, the branchlines of the old LNWR to Morecambe Euston Road and especially to Glasson Dock were relative backwaters. The daily monotony of ex-LMS 0-4-4 tank engines on the shuttle between Euston Road and Lancaster Castle was broken each morning and evening by the Up and Down Ulster Express, with its *Princess Coronation* or similar express locomotive hauling the train between Euston and Promenade, and the more work-a-day Belfast Boat Express with its *Black 5* to and from Manchester.

The summer saw its fair share of excursions bringing an increasing variety of locomotives of all sizes. The Glasson Dock branch, in comparison, saw only the occasional goods working to the quays alongside the Lancaster Canal basin and the mouth of the Lune. The section of the branch within Lancaster itself saw more goods traffic to Messrs Williamson's linoleum mills, the LMR Engineer's yard, and onto St Georges Quay and, until the late 50's, Lancaster Gasworks. For the Pearsall brothers, their attention was drawn to the former branch. The latter lines were largely ignored, one significant exception being when a rail tour ventured down to Glasson Dock in 1954.

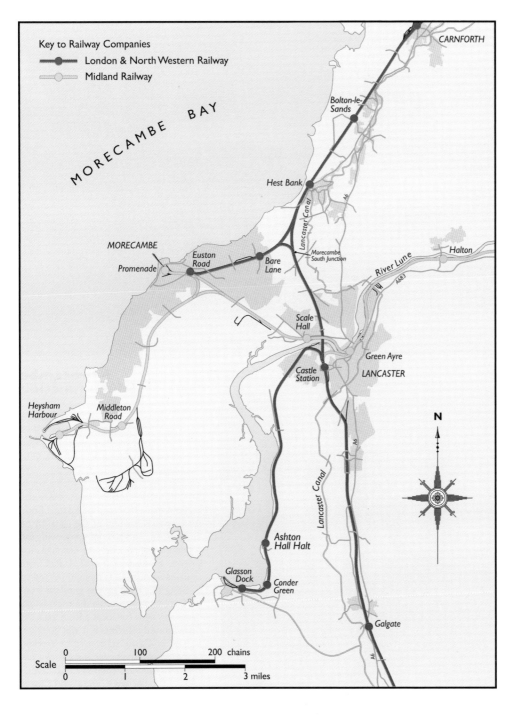

Hest Bank

PEA256
undated, probably 1952
An unidentified ex-LMS Fowler 2-6-4T eases train W509 onto the branch at Hest Bank bound for Morecambe. The fireman has a brief chat with the boys who have ventured through the fence onto the lineside. To the left are the vast sands and salt marshes of Morecambe Bay, whilst in the background is Warton Crag with its limestone quarry, more often a feature of photographs taken at nearby Carnforth.
The leading carriages on the train are ex-LNER Gresley designs suggesting this is an excursion from the north-east via Stainmore and that the loco has taken over the train at Tebay.

PEB736
26th August 1953
With Morecambe being a popular resort close to the Lake District and few of its visitors arriving by car, it is not surprising that the railways ran summer services to Lake Side and the Windermere steamers. Bringing the excursionists back to their boarding houses and hotels, ex-LMS Stanier 4MT 2-6-4T 42589 takes the branch to Morecambe with the 5-45pm from Lakeside. Whether the train was packed or it was just a fun thing to do, the guard has allowed a boy and girl to look out of the window of the leading brake third. Such is the angle chosen by the photographer; it is possible to see through the station to the water troughs beyond.

Morecambe South Junction

PEB670
1st August 1953
As seen in other photographs in this album, the Lancaster Castle to Morecambe Euston Road shuttles were usually made up of a loco with a set of three non-corridor carriages. Here the 2-30pm from Morecambe Euston Road to Crewe is formed of the usual three carriage set and strengthened with the addition of six corridor carriages for Crewe. Ex-LMS 2P 0-4-4T 41904 from Green Ayre shed is being thrashed to bring this train up the gradient from Bare Lane and onto the main line, a popular sight for local enthusiasts. As mentioned elsewhere, it will be taken off at Castle station, to be worked forward by whichever locomotive has previously piloted train W254 between Barrow Central and Castle.

Bare Lane

PEO031
9th September 1950

Ex-LMS 4MT Fowler 2-6-4T 42321 comes off the single line from Hest Bank and into Bare Lane with train W519, an excursion from Barrow to Morecambe. Excited excursionists, perhaps heading to see the illuminations, lean out of the windows of the motley collection of carriages. Whilst most are non-corridor carriages, the seventh and eighth appear to be corridor stock with recessed end doors; the leading carriage is still annotated LMS.

PEJ635
8th September 1956

BR 4MT 2-6-0 76024 rounds the curve from Hest Bank to Bare Lane with train 509, an excursion from Saltburn to Morecambe. Unusually, the West Auckland 4MT has worked beyond Tebay, perhaps due to the lack of a spare LMR loco. Whatever the reason, it caused quite a stir among the local enthusiasts. The train is largely made up of ex-LNER Gresley-style carriages.

PEK292
26th May 1958

The 9-45am through goods train from Farrington Junction to Heysham via Morecambe Promenade rolls onto Bare Lane junction pulled by WD 2-8-0 90375. As ever with trains between Heysham and the Preston area, there is a brake van behind the loco as well as at the rear of the train, thus facilitating reversal.

Bare Lane

PEB237
12th April 1953

In April 1953 the track at Bare Lane level crossing was re-laid and the road surface rebuilt with a tar macadam surface. By the time LMS-design Fairburn 4MT 2-6-4T 42135 enters Bare Lane with the 2-30pm Sundays Only shuttle from Morecambe Euston Road to Lancaster Castle, single line working is in operation on the Down line, which is almost complete, and the workmen have turned their attention to the Up line. Curiously, in the original print, a road roller is visible belonging to Johnson Bros. (Aylesford) Ltd. of Vale Road, Tonbridge, Kent. Unlike today, there is a total absence of cars parked along South Road, to the left of the railway.

PEJ839
16th June 1957
A pair of the West Cumberland BR Derby Lightweight DMUs, led by M79609, pulls away from Bare Lane. They form train W527, a Morecambe to Llandudno excursion. The West Cumberland units were fitted with bars across the windows which allowed their use over the Maryport & Carlisle section, with its restricted clearances.

Morecambe Euston Road

PEO029
8th August 1950

Train W252, the midday departure to Manchester, leaves platform 3 at Euston Road with ex-LMS 5MT *Crab* 2-6-0 42711 at the head. The train of non–corridor carriages is crossing onto the Up Main line. The points in the foreground allowed trains to run from the Down Main line onto the connecting line to Promenade station. Behind the photographer this track becomes York Siding.

A68-04-2
4th March 1968

With only 5 months left of scheduled steam trains from Carnforth shed, BR Sulzer Type 2 D5170 leads an unidentified BR 9F 2-10-0 with the 12-12pm fuel oil train from Heysham Moss Sidings to Neville Hill. Whilst the diesel is half way through its short life the 9F will soon be withdrawn, both having a 14-year service life. One or both of the locos will have run around at Promenade before heading the train to Carnforth and over the Furness & Midland line to Wennington where the pre-1967 route will be rejoined. The redundant Euston Road signal box stands at left, the signal gantry here having been removed, but some of the point work giving access to Euston Road station is still in place.

PEZ933
5th April 1967

Brush Type 4 D1633 heads way from Morecambe with the first run of train 3A41, the Heysham to Camden Freightliner. Heysham first handled modern, international standard container traffic in 1958 but it was the introduction of BR's Freightliner brand from 1965 that saw the dedicated Heysham service being introduced. Euston Road signalbox is still open with the former LNWR station being used as carriage sidings, especially in the Summer season.

Morecambe Euston Road

PEK446
14th September 1958

One of the last trains from Euston Road in its role as a fully-fledged passenger station; ex-LMS 5MT 4-6-0 45306 awaits the signal to start the 7-10pm Sundays Only train to Manchester from platform 4. From the following day and for the next four years Euston Road will be open in the summer season only. Our photographer is taking advantage of the elevation of Euston Road signal box. Note the number of motor coaches in the station car park – also location of the Ribble bus depot since 1936 (land acquired from BR in 1953). Since Ribble is a part of BET, of which the British Transport Commission and BR are significant shareholders (as successors to the LMS), this is not an unsurprising occurrence.

PEA320
undated, 1968

Unlike its Midland neighbour, the former LNWR station at Morecambe was handy for the town but not for the seafront. It had opened in 1888 and closed from 15th September 1958. Such was the popularity of Morecambe that it was retained as an excursion station to relieve Promenade during summer and illuminations seasons, the last working day being 8th September 1962. Although plans were made to again use Euston Road on Saturdays only for the 1963 summer season, this was cancelled at a fairly late stage. It remained, trainless, in the public summer timetables during 1964 also. Here we see Euston Road in the years after closure to excursion trains; track has been removed, platforms four and five demolished and the signal box closed with some windows already removed. The goods yard, however, remains open at this time.

PEI664
16th August 1968

Following a derailment of ICI tank wagons, BR Clayton Type 1 D8522 stands on the Down line at the entrance to Promenade station. One of the derailed wagons has been placed to the side of the tracks in the ballast with its buffer beams propped up with sleepers. The Lancashire County Council fire engine is in attendance due to the highly inflammable nature of the tank contents. Interestingly, on 31st July 1968 the 06-40 block fuel train from Heysham Moss Sidings to Rowley Regis had derailed at this same spot, overturning several 100 ton oil tank wagons. The Clayton locomotives (soon to receive TOPS Class 17) were among the most distinctive of the BR Type 1s, with their centre cab complete with inset for single line tablet apparatus. Rolled out from Messrs Clayton Engineering in June 1963, D8522 had a very short life in service like its sisters. It was withdrawn in October 1968 to be laid up in Glasgow until removal to the scrap yard in June 1972.

Glasson Dock

PEF827
1st May 1954

Ex-LMS 4MT Fowler 2-6-4T 42316 with carriages from train W699, the MLS/SLS *North Lancashire Railtour*. This train was an afternoon excursion from Preston visiting Longridge, Pilling, Glasson Dock, the Hincaster branch and Lancaster Old station. 42316 is seen here during the shunting required to run around its train. It had to push the front three of its six carriages out as far as the curve from Conder Green and the Conder viaduct in order to then not only run around the rear three carriages but also shunt them into a siding before collecting the front three again, running around those, pulling them out of the yard and then running back to couple up the rear three. Note the contrast in clothing of the women, in their over-large overcoats, to the gent in his sports jacket and tie. The three carriages seen here are M816M (a 12-wheel ex-LNWR Saloon of 1913), M822M (ex-LMS Manchester – Blackpool "Club" train Saloon of 1935) and M823M (Saloon, from the ex-LMS *Coronation Scot* set of 1939 that went to the USA).

PEF828
1st May 1954

Train W699, the MLS/SLS *North Lancashire Railtour,* leaves Glasson Dock after much shunting and delay, and is here crossing the salt marsh on the approach to the Conder viaduct and Conder Green station. The carriages behind 42316 and M823M, M822M and M816M are M809M (ex-MR, 1910, "semi royal"), M815M (ex-LNWR 8-wheel Saloon of 1908) and (out of shot) M818M (ex-LMS saloon of 1925). All the shunting at Glasson Dock, and earlier at Pilling, meant that the train arrived back in Preston at 11-15pm! Some of the stock had seen use on the famous pre-war Manchester – Blackpool "Club" trains and were used from 1951 on the weekday "Land Cruise" trains from Llandudno and Rhyl around North Wales.

Lancaster

PEQ062
25th May 1951

Linoleum was one of Lancaster's major products through much of the twentieth century, having made James Williamson a millionaire in earlier years through his factory alongside the Lune. Over three years since Nationalisation, ex-LMS 4F 0-6-0 4032 still sports LMS livery as it shunts Williamson's wharf sidings off the Glasson Dock branch. The weather is good and the tarpaulin used to protect the crew from the elements has been rolled onto the cab roof.

Lancaster Castle

PEG359
13th April 1955

The Royal tour of Lancashire: having completed ceremonial duties in Lancaster, the Queen and Duke of Edinburgh have returned to the Royal Train at Castle station. Here ex-LMS 5MT 4-6-0s 45425 and 45454 head it away from Castle station and through the crowds of onlookers lining the track. Another 5MT 4-6-0, 45072, stands in the sidings as the train passes. Note the unusual van above the tender of 45425 with what appear to be archaic oil lamp housings in the roof. As well as lining the tracks near No 2 signal box, the crowds are still gathered on Meeting House Lane and Wheatfield Street to watch the Royal party leave the city. Whilst the continuing popularity of the Monarch still attracts such crowds, it is doubtful if the authorities would allow such casual access to the tracks, let alone to the Royal party.

Eight - A Miscellany

TO COMMEMORATE the Queen's Coronation in 1953, the British Transport Commission organised a travelling exhibition entitled *Royal Journey*. Royal Train artefacts, including carriages from past Royal trains were on display. The first destination was Battersea Wharf goods station, London, from 19th June to 11th July. It then proceeded to be displayed at Birmingham, Llandudno, Chester General, Morecambe Promenade, Edinburgh Waverley, Dundee West, Glasgow St Enoch, Leeds City (South), Sheffield Midland, Nottingham London Road, Plymouth Millbay, Bristol Temple Meads and Cardiff General before finishing its tour at Wolverton on 22nd November. Morecambe played host to the exhibition from 17th to 20th August, coinciding with the resumption of electric trains on the Lancaster – Morecambe – Heysham route on the 17th.

On 13th April 1955 Her Majesty the Queen and Prince Philip undertook a two-day tour of Lancashire. Their tour commenced in Morecambe, before proceeding by car to Lancaster. Here they visited the Castle and Shire Hall, met staff of the Duchy and received a civic welcome at the Town Hall. The first day of the tour also included Preston, the Lancashire Police Headquarters at Hutton, Southport and Blackpool. A Royal Performance was held at the Blackpool Opera House to a full house despite tickets being priced at 5 guineas! On the following day the Royal party visited Darwen, Blackburn and Nelson.

The Midland Railway's harbour at Heysham of 1904 not only replaced its predecessor at Morecambe but also took passenger sailings away from Barrow's Ramsden Dock station and later from Fleetwood to become the main English port for services to Northern Ireland. As well as the well-known passenger ferries, a number of smaller work boats operated in and around the Heysham; all of interest to the Pearsall brothers.

Morecambe Promenade

PEB728
18th August 1953
"New" Lancaster – Morecambe – Heysham electric motor car M28221M stands in Platform 3 alongside ex-Caledonian Railway 4-2-2 123 with its Royal Train Pilot headboard at the head of the exhibition train in Platform 2. Between Platforms 2 and 3 was a rockery adding some colour to this attractive station.

Morecambe Promenade

PEB733
18th August 1953

CR 4-2-2 123 in Platform 2, ahead of the ex-LNWR 1903 Royal saloon. As well as the loco and carriages with royal connections, several locomotive headboards from past Royal Trains were also exhibited. Above the tender can be seen the headboard from the "Honeymoon" Royal Train of the then Princess Elizabeth and Philip Mountbatten from 1947. Note the water column behind the release road bufferstops. From the amount of ash between the rails, it must have been common for loco crews to service their locos on arrival rather than wait until they were released and run to the turntable.

PEB729
18th August 1953

Queen Adelaide's saloon No 2 of the London & Birmingham railway was exhibited on an ex-LMS *lowmac* wagon, coupled to Queen Victoria's saloon of the LNWR. Tarpaulins were strung from the platform canopy to screen off the exhibits whilst keeping Platform 1 available. Despite it being high summer the older visitors are wrapped up in their overcoats.

PEB730
18th August 1953

Queen Victoria's saloon, in LNWR livery, is coupled next to one of the later ex-LNWR Royal Saloons built for her heir, Edward VII, and painted in LMS wartime livery.

Morecambe Promenade

PEF991
13th April 1955

The Royal Train stands in Platform 1 behind ex-LMS 5MT 4-6-0s 45425 and 45454 from Springs Branch shed. Since the Royal party will travel by road to Lancaster the train is now an empty carriage working. 45425 has lost its Royal Train head lamp code and carries reporting number W700. When originally electrified, catenary covered all the platform roads at Promenade. With the upgrading of the system from 6.6KV 25Hertz to 6.6KV 50Hz, the wires were removed from Platforms 1 and 2 and the heavy catenary gantries over Platform 1 were removed, as seen here.

Heysham Harbour

PEN080
1st September 1946
The LMS built the Class WT 2-6-4T locomotives at its Derby works and shipped them in component parts to its Northern Counties Committee subsidiary in Northern Ireland. Here NCC No 7 sits on the deck of LMS TSS *Slieve Bloom* awaiting departure for Belfast.

PEA018
22nd August 1947
Part-dismantled LMS-NCC WT Class 2-6-4T No 4 on a well wagon after arrival on the quayside at Heysham. Withdrawn in 1970, this locomotive is preserved by the Railway Preservation Society of Ireland at Whitehead, Co. Antrim.

PES056
1949
The Sligo Leitrim & Northern Counties Railway bought two 0-6-4Ts on hire purchase from Beyer Peacock of Manchester, the last traditional steam locomotives to be built for a railway in the Irish Republic. The partly dismantled locomotive, either *Lough Erne* or *Lough Melvin,* awaits loading onto one of the BR cargo vessels bound for Belfast.

PEW054
1st July 1951
Ulster Transport Authority WT 2-6-4T No.54 being loaded onto one of the BR cargo vessels, on its way from Derby to Belfast. Number 54 will see active service until April 1967. The UTA had taken over the former NCC lines from the British Transport Commission in 1949.

Heysham Harbour

PEB138
31st December 1952
Myles Kennedy and *Red Nab* dredging the entrance to Heysham harbour. *Myles Kennedy*, a bucket dredger, had been built for the Furness Railway by Messrs Fleming & Ferguson of Paisley in 1921. The 413 ton dredger, Official Number 146021, originally worked in the channels leading to Barrow Docks but was moved to Heysham in 1927. She was superseded at Barrow by the new LMS dredger *Piel*. *Red Nab* had been built for the Midland Railway in 1908 by Messrs W Simons & Co. of Renfrew. The 537 ton steam hopper barge was registered at Lancaster, O.N. 128311, and worked at Heysham until replaced by a vessel of the same name in July 1960.

PEB141
31st December 1952
Berthed alongside the North Quay is another ex-Midland Railway veteran, the *Laga*. She had been built in 1901 by J & K Smit at Kinderdijk, Netherlands but the Midland did not acquire her until 1905 when she was registered at Lancaster, O.N.10155. After fifty years service at Heysham, in December 1955, *Laga* will be replaced by the *Laga B* and sold to Messrs R. Abel & Sons Ltd. for use on the Mersey. She will be renamed *Lunesdale* and work as a suction hopper dredger before being broken up early in 1968.

PEK724
4th August 1959
Dredging the entrance to Heysham harbour. The *Myles Kennedy* is discharging into the hopper barge *Laga B* whilst another dredger, possibly the *Hessam* [although our catalogue says *Pendennis*] dredges alongside. The *Laga B* had been built for BR London Midland Region by Messrs. Ferguson Brothers of Port Glasgow in 1955, replacing the *Laga*.
The author has been unable to establish any information regarding a dredger named *Pendennis* other than it is unlikely to have been a railway-owned vessel. It is suspected to be more than likely the ex MR dredger *Hessam*.

PEK748
6th August 1959

The tug *Wyvern* guides *Duke of Lancaster* away from Heysham. The *Wyvern* was built for the Midland Railway in 1905 as a tug / tender for use at Heysham. From 1908 until the Second World War, she was predominantly used on passenger excursions within Morecambe Bay, often running to Fleetwood. BR used her solely as a tug, as seen here, until withdrawing her in June 1960 for cutting up. The *Duke of Lancaster* was at the other end of the passenger vessel hierarchy. She was built for BR by Messrs. Harland and Wolff of Belfast in 1956 for use on the overnight Belfast service alongside sister ships *Duke of Argyll* and *Duke of Rothesay*, one of which can be seen at her berth in this photograph. *Duke of Lancaster* had additionally been fitted out for occasional use as a cruise ship and could be found taking cruises from Heysham to various points around Europe until 1966. From that year she was permanently required on the Belfast run as the *Duke of Rothesay* was reallocated to the Fishguard to Rosslare route.

PEI798
25th September 1971

Duke of Lancaster as a car ferry. She had been converted in early 1970, when doors were added at the stern and part of the main deck altered to carry 105 cars. She would continue in service from Heysham until the general withdrawal of passenger services to Belfast after 5th April 1975. After a period on the Fishguard to Rosslare and Holyhead to Dun Laoghaire services, her last run in service was on 17th January 1979 when she sailed to Barrow to be laid up. Seven months later she sailed to the Welsh side of the river Dee to be converted into a "retail and entertainment" venture. The venture was short-lived and she still lies in a somewhat sorry state, concreted in to the river bank at Llanerch y Mor, near Mostyn.

Carnforth

PEJ538
11th August 1956

Looking north from the Furness & Midland line, ex-LMS 6P Jubilee 4-6-0 45563 *Australia* coasts into Carnforth with train W432, the 10-50am from Glasgow Central to Liverpool Exchange. The train is passing Carnforth North Ground Frame (seen beneath the gantry), the two sidings adjacent to the main line, with a water crane between, being Down loops created during World War Two. The old fog signalman's hut adjacent to the Up line is in remarkable condition with its stable door and hatch covers.

Nine - Carnforth

IN THE DAYS before West Coast Railways, Steamtown and the closure of the main line station, Carnforth was a major interchange between Furness, West Yorkshire and the main line to Carlisle, Lancaster and beyond. Most main line expresses whistled through Carnforth station whilst local services to Barrow or Whitehaven occasionally made connection with those which did stop here rather than at Lancaster. Those curiosities of the pre-Beeching era, the through carriages to and from Leeds and Bradford (having left the main Morecambe-bound trains at Wennington) started from and terminated here, making connection with the Furness and Lancaster & Carlisle line trains.

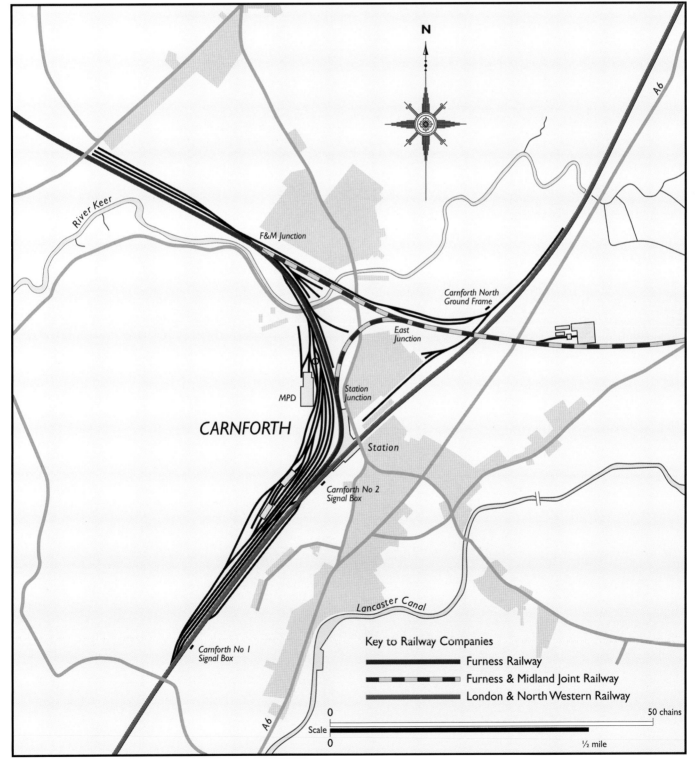

Carnforth, Netherbeck Farm

PEF934
25th October 1954
Ex-LMS 3MT 2-6-2T 40011 heads east with the 2-43pm train from Carnforth to Leeds City (North). The Carnforth shed loco will take this pair of carriages as far as Wennington where they will be shunted to form the rear section of a similarly timed train from Morecambe Promenade to Leeds and Bradford Forster Square. The signal wire in the cess is for Carnforth East Junction Down Distant signal.

Carnforth East Junction

PEF981
19th March 1956
The 1-55pm through carriages from Leeds City (North) to Carnforth cross the Lancaster & Carlisle main line, hauled by ex-LMS 5MT 4-6-0 44892. The West Coast Main Line, with its loops, passes under the right hand span, whilst those to the left are sidings into the storage depot on the erstwhile Ironworks site. These are accessed via a reversal from East Junction, to the left of this view. The roofs seen above the Furness & Midland line belong to the former Midland Railway roundhouse.

PEF979
19th March 1955
Ex-LMS Stanier 4MT 2-6-4T 42432 accelerates away from East Junction with the 2-43pm train from Carnforth to Leeds City (North). Once the Carnforth loco has shunted the train into the bay at Wennington, it will return to Carnforth with through carriages from a Leeds to Morecambe Promenade train. The condemned wagons on the right are stood in the "top end" sidings, alongside the spur from East Junction to the old Carnforth Ironworks site, used by various businesses and still served by rail at this time.

PEF978
19th March 1955
The 10-15am Class J goods from Stourton to Carnforth with ex-LMS 4F 0-6-0 44562 at its head rolls across Carnforth East junction heading for F&M Yard. Photographer Pearsall is standing at the top of East Junction signal box steps with the direct line to F&M Junction, and its connection to the line on to Barrow, at left with the sharp curve round to the passenger station to the right. The former MR roundhouse can be seen in the distance.

Carnforth F&M yard

PEF999
23th April 1955
Fifty-five year old ex-Midland 3F 0-6-0 43257 starts a through goods train from the Furness & Midland yard towards East Junction, bound for Skipton. Meanwhile, an unidentified 2-6-4T is held at the signal with another goods train on the through line. To the left, beyond the under bridge, is the site of the original Midland Railway loco shed before being replaced in 1874 by the roundhouse a half a mile further east along the F&M line.

Carnforth F&M Junction

PEF995
19th April 1955
Ex-Midland 4F 0-6-0 43871 based at Stourton shed sets back a goods train along the Furness Down Line towards F&M Junction and into the sidings beyond. The 4F has a full tender of coal, suggesting it is not long off Carnforth shed and has been brought out to shunt this particular train. The flat area alongside the train was the site of Carnforth F&M Junction passenger station, where trains off the Furness & Midland Joint line from Wennington connected with the Furness Railway services from 1868 until the direct curve from East Junction into Carnforth Joint station was opened in 1880.

Carnforth

PEJ541
11th August 1956
Ex-LMS 6P *Jubilee* 4-6-0 45719 *Glorious* stands at Carnforth No. 2 Up Home signal with the 8-40am from Dundee to Liverpool Exchange train whilst ex-LMS Stanier 4MT 2-6-4T 42544 accelerates away from Carnforth with the 1-37pm from Crewe to Windermere. The Windermere train is passing the site of Carnforth No. 3 box, closed in 1939. The line coming in from the left is the spur leading from East Junction and the F&M yard, down alongside the LCR main line where sidings back into the former Ironworks site. Whilst there is a visible link with the LCR via the two wartime Down loops, this spur was never used for trains from Furness to the north. Beyond the railway is the A6, then the main road from the Midlands and North West to Carlisle and Glasgow. Very few vehicles can be seen!

Carnforth
Station Junction

PEJ139
3rd June 1955
Although introduced onto services in West Cumberland at the end of 1954, DMUs were not regularly seen on services on the Furness line south of Whitehaven until the mid 1960s. An exception to the rule is seen here on the on the sixth day of the 1955 rail strike. A pair of Derby Lightweight DMUs, led by unit M79008, are leaving Carnforth with the 2-30pm strike service from Preston to Workington. A pair of be-suited managers are in the cab and it is hard to tell whether the driver is also management.

Carnforth

PEJ543
11th August 1956
Waiting for the guard's whistle is ex-LMS 4MT Fowler 2-6-4T 42313 with the 5-45pm train from Windermere to Morecambe made up of a mix of 3 non-corridor carriages followed by four or more corridor carriages. A set of Scottish Region ex-LMS carriages stands in the adjacent bay platform, perhaps waiting to form a return Morecambe Promenade to Glasgow Central train.

PEJ668
Sunday 14th October 1956
The 11-15am from Birmingham New Street to Glasgow Central passes Carnforth No 2 box behind ex-LMS 8P *Princess Coronation* 4-6-2 46225 *Duchess of Gloucester*. The train is running wrong line due to engineering works that day. From this vantage point at the end of Platforms 3 and 4, the bridge from the former LNWR railwaymen's cottages at Grosvenor Place to the site of that company's loco shed can be seen in the distance.

PEF985
2nd April 1955
In the mid 1950s Barrow had one of the best Rugby League teams in Britain, with several members of the Great Britain squad playing for them. 1955 was a particularly good year when they beat local rivals Workington in the Challenge Cup Finals at Wembley. Prior to that, Barrow played Hunslet at Central Park, Wigan. To accommodate the fans on their journey to Wigan, two private charter trains or "Parspecs" were run. Here ex-LMS 5MT 4-6-0 45193 accelerates away from Carnforth station with train W526, the 10-50am from Barrow Central to Wigan North Western. In the bay platform stands ex-LMS 5MT 4-6-0 45240 with the 8-35am parcels from Carlisle to Crewe.

PEF986
2nd April 1955
The second "Parspec" left Barrow Central at 11-22am for the Rugby League Challenge Cup Semi-final and is seen from No 2 signal box. Train W528 with ex-LMS 5MT 4-6-0 45454 from Springs Branch at the head pulls out onto the LCR main line. Two weeks later 45454, with its white-painted smokebox hinges and buffers, would be seen on another special, hauling the Royal train during the Queen's official visit to Lancashire.

Carnforth No.2

PEK395
25th July 1958
Ex-LMS 7P *Rebuilt Scot* 7P 4-6-0 46106 *Gordon Highlander* approaches Carnforth No. 2 signal box with the 3-50pm Fridays Only train from Crewe to Glasgow Central. 46106 was unique among the rebuilt *Scots* in having straight sided smoke deflectors instead of the smaller angular deflectors fitted to the other members of the class. The Shell-BP tank wagons are probably en-route to or from the Trimpell refinery at Heysham Moss.

Carnforth MPD

PEI666
undated, probably 16th August 1968

In the week after the last BR steam-hauled train ran, Carnforth MPD became something of a mausoleum with locos filling the shed yard. There is no point putting tarpaulins over their chimneys as the recently active engines are stored, awaiting their last journey to the scrapyard. Looking down over the scene at the north end of Carnforth shed we can see ex-LMS 5MT 4-6-0s with their different types of boiler, including 44877, 44963, 44758, 45200, plus BR 4MT 4-6-0 75048, kept clean by enthusiasts in its last days in steam, and 9F 92051. In some cases the locos had seen service up until 4th August whilst others have already lost their smokebox number plates and shed plates to collectors.

PEI667
16th August 1968

Looking over the north end of Carnforth shed yard towards the passenger station and the town beyond, ex-LMS 5MTs 4-6-0 44709 and 44802 stand with their piston rods already disconnected ready for the final journey. On the adjacent tracks are signs of the future. For a short period after closure as a steam shed, Carnforth remained open as a diesel depot; unidentified diesels of Type 2 and Type 4 stand outside the shed. Further over, signs of the future at Carnforth shed are already apparent. In readiness for it becoming Steamtown, four BR-built locos were brought to Carnforth. Fairburn 2-6-4Ts 42085 and 42073, Ivatt Class 2MT 2-6-0 46441 and Thompson B1 61306 stand under the footbridge alongside some 4MT 4-6-0s, including 75027. In the siding adjacent to the passenger station stands a line of scrap locos, partly hidden behind a rake of carriages and wagons.

Index

Acknowledgements

I would like to thank Peter Robinson for advising on the selection of photographs from the Cumbrian Railways Association's Pearsall Collection and preparing them for publication. Additionally my thanks go to Mike Peascod for his technical preparation of this book, Howard Quayle for reviewing the text, Alan Johnstone for preparing the maps and to fellow CRA members and friends on the Association's chat group for helping me clear a few points. On the Internet the Six Bells Junction web site proved useful in filling out details of the *North Lancashire Railtour*.

Sources and Select Reading

Anyone wanting to know more about the history of the railways covered in this book will find much in the following books.

A Regional History of the Railways of Great Britain, The North West by GO Holt, ISBN 0-946537-34-8   David & Charles, 1978
The Lancaster and Preston Junction Railway by MD Greville and GO Holt, David & Charles, 1961
The Little North Western Railway by D Binns, ISBN 0-907941-01-X, Locomotives International, 1982
The 'Little' North Western Railway by M Bairstow, ISBN 1-871944-21-X, Author, 2000
Railways around Lancaster by K Nuttall and T Rawlings, ISBN 0-852065-78-7, Dalesman, 1980

Back Cover
Bolton-le-Sands
PEK195
6th April 1958
The Down line is being relaid to the south of Bolton-le-Sands station and ex-LMS 4MT Fowler 2-6-4T 42301 pauses during ballasting. It carries a Class K head code indicating its role on a ballast train on a short haul run.

Morecambe South Junction
PEJ633
8th September 1956
Thundering up the grade onto the main line is ex-LMS 2P 0-4-4T 41904 with the 2-25pm from Morecambe Euston Road to Crewe, train W266. The original allocation of two of these small locos would stay on at Green Ayre to work the Lancaster – Morecambe shuttles until 1959, when they were withdrawn and sent to Barrow for scrapping.

Bolton-le-Sands
PEJ988
8th September 1957
Ex-LMS 5MT 2-6-0 42955 is about to pass under Pasture Lane with an Up "Maltese Cross" goods. There are four fitted vans at the head, as required to allow the train to run under a Class E express goods headcode.

Claughton Manor
PEF957
18th January 1955
Ex-LMS *Crab* 5MT 2-6-0 42810 passes along the snow-covered Lune valley with the 8-33am train from Bradford Forster Square to Morecambe Promenade. The train is passing the siding into the West End brickworks of the Claughton Brick and Tile Company. Beyond the signal is Claughton Manor signal box and the siding into Claughton Manor Brick and Tile Company's Manor Brick and Tile works. The signal is Claughton Manor's Down advance starter, protecting the siding, with the Distant for Lane Foot Level Crossing sharing the same signal post.

Lancaster, Barley Cop Lane
PEB222
27th March 1953
BR Peppercorn A1 4-6-2 60161 *North British* heads out of the Lancaster suburb of Skerton with train W67, the 11-25am Birmingham New Street to Glasgow Central. The leading full brake, with its panelling from the early days of the LMS, seems odd against what is otherwise a fairly uniform modern train of late LMS-design stock. The signals in the distance are an Intermediate Block signal controlled from Morecambe South Junction and the Down Distant signal for that junction.